CW01034018

Hospital Ship

Hospital Ship

*Memories of HMHS Tjitjalengka
During World War II*

Jack Woolman

Brewin Books

First published by Brewin Books Ltd,
Doric House, 56 Alcester Road, Studley,
Warwickshire B80 7LG in 2001.
www.brewinbooks.com

ISBN 1 85858 197 4

A Cataloguing in Publication Record
for this title is available from
the British Library.

Typeset in Times
Printed in Great Britain
by SupaPrint (Redditch) Limited.
www.supaprint.com

TABLE OF CONTENTS

Jack Woolman in 1941.

Chapter 1-

CALL UP

I left school at fifteen, and my father had to buy me out, because I was supposed to go on until I was seventeen and then possibly to university. The school was King Edward's, then on its original site in New Street, Birmingham. During the next five years I worked in the family firm, which was begun by my Grandfather. I was the third generation in the business, a mail order firm selling mainly Chrysanthemums.

During those five years the shadow of Hitler loomed ever larger and more menacing. I decided that I ought to read *Mein Kampf*, which he had written just a few years before, so that I would form my own opinion of him. Many people were certain that his intention was to conquer first Europe, then Russia and eventually the rest of the world. Many other people were just as sure that he simply wanted to free Germany from the restrictions and loss of territory that ensued from the Great War 1914 -1918. A few years passed and from time to time he annexed various territories and countries and afterwards, when the other European countries became frightened and threatened him (still with the usual "pro" and "anti" people), he became very pleasant and assured them that he had no more plans to expand in Europe. The various governments accepted that and left him to continue with his plans, although everyone was now getting more scared. I can't really blame the governments for this because so many people remembered the war twenty years before and just didn't want another one. I read his book and felt that he had expressed just what he was going to do and how he was going to do it. Although in the carefree days of youth you don't worry too much about the future, *Mein Kampf* impressed me so much that I still was very suspicious of him as things developed. When Prime Minister Chamberlain flew back from Munich with his famous bit of paper which was going to mean peace in our time and Hitler afterwards continued with his plans of expansion, I was certain that we were going to have to go to war against him. It seemed the only possible conclusion because he was continuing to threaten surrounding countries, such as when he occupied Czechoslovakia, and was building up his war machine at a terrific rate. What he reported as cruisers, within the size and power to which he was restricted, were actually far over that and virtually battleships. He trained men to be glider pilots (or so he said) who in due course were in his air force. In Britain there were statements made by his supporters trying to persuade us that he wasn't doing all of those things and would never attack us. We even heard that most of his hundreds of tanks were just cardboard models built to confuse us. Such was his propaganda. There were many other tales of a similar kind, the aim being to lull us into a sense of security whilst he carried out his real plans. Obviously this was going to affect everyone including me – so what should I do about it? I was just at the age for an early call up to the forces.

The first decision I made was that I would have to go when my call came. I was never in favour of being a conscientious objector. It just didn't appeal to me. What I felt I did want, was to try to enlist into some section where I would have beneficial experience and knowledge which would be of use to me after the war was over, if I survived. From the time of the beginning of hostilities every thought of "after the war", and there were many, was qualified by that.

My instinct was to get into the medical section. I felt that it would be valuable knowledge for the rest of my life. Within that was the use of my photographic expertise, which at that time was in its early stages. My plans were to improve by studying it. This was not difficult as it was my main hobby and had been since I first processed my own photos when I was nine. I bought a better enlarger and practised. The medical side was a matter of building a background that would enable me to apply for this section of the armed forces. The next question was which arm, Navy, Army or Air Force? I leant towards the Navy because my father was a signalman in it during the First World War and all my life I had been hearing "You ought to have been in the Navy!" Particularly when I didn't eat all my food, it always finished "I've seen ships go down carrying food to us." Sadly it didn't have any effect on my eating habits. I just didn't understand then. Later I did. I decided to take a few certificates in first aid and home nursing and other allied subjects. I went to my Doctor, Dr Quinet in Solihull and his wife who was also a Doctor. They taught me and then I took the various examinations, which I passed. I was in that way able to ask for the naval medical section when called up.

At that time I wrote to the RAF for information on what they could offer me if I volunteered instead of waiting to be called up. I told them my interests and in due course they replied telling me of the position, which basically was that they wanted all sorts and would offer anything.

Thus by the middle of 1939 I had done all I could to perhaps influence the pattern of my life should the war happen. Personally I was sure it would and I felt it would start in autumn 1939 after the harvest was gathered in, I wasn't far out. Gradually the situation developed and preparations were made for the outbreak of hostilities. Hitler eventually invaded Poland. We gave him an ultimatum. Either cease-fire and withdraw from Poland or we shall declare war.

On the 3rd of September 1939 at 11 o'clock the Prime Minister Neville Chamberlain addressed the people of Britain. That morning my father and I were showing a keen chrysanthemum exhibitor, Mr. Molyneaux, who was head gardener of Hewell Grange, Bromsgrove, round our exhibition chrysanthemums. We timed it so we could get down to our house to hear it. After a preamble Chamberlain said, "We gave Hitler an ultimatum that unless we heard that he had withdrawn from Poland by 11:00 o'clock today Britain would be at war with Germany. There has been no response to that and therefore we are now at war." There was a long pause whilst it sank in and then Mr, Molyneaux said "Ah, silly ain't it!" There were many times during the next six years when I remembered that statement.

Not many minutes after the speech the air raid sirens went off and everyone thought that it had begun. The sirens howled, the air raid wardens alerted themselves and several of these who were detailed so to do cycled round the roads blowing their officially distributed whistles and shouted to anyone who was about to "take cover". It was a false alarm and things gradually settled down again. I felt that the world would never be the same again, although I couldn't foresee just what changes there would be. It was not long, however, before some began to show. On that Sunday night they played jazz music over the radio (no TV, of course). Up until then no popular music had been allowed, only classical or church type. Another surprise was that when the air alarm had been sounded there was suddenly a whole lot of what we later learned to call barrage balloons up in the sky, each tethered to the ground by a long cable. Up until then they had only been stored on the ground and we didn't know they were there. Their purpose was to provide a screen of cables around cities and other sensitive places to prevent the German dive-bombers from performing. These were planes that screamed down almost to the ground level and when they were almost there, aiming with the flight of the plane itself, they loosed a bomb as they swung up again. If they came too close they hit a cable.

The next day everyone went about their business as usual but not really knowing what was going to happen or when. Would our jobs be safe? Would we have to face air raids? When would we be called up? And a hundred worries of that kind; in fact nothing really happened and Hitler carried on his war with Poland.

When we declared war we were expecting our various allied countries to do the same. France said she was joining us later in the day and we expected the Commonwealth to join too. They all did except South Africa, which for a while held debates in their parliament as to whether or not they should. This was really the Boers against the English South Africans. After a while the argument was settled and the war supporters won. In fact it was a good thing that they did so. What would have happened if we had not had the use of ports like Cape Town and Durban, I hate to think. The colonies, and there were many of them in all parts of the world, were under our control and we used them as we wanted. I well remember being quite surprised that South Africa didn't join us straight away.

Everything at home was in turmoil. Imagine that you had been following a pattern for most of your life and suddenly the bottom dropped out. You didn't know what was going to happen next. Were there going to be any air raids? If there were what was it going to be like? What was the use of growing plants for retail sales? My own inclination was to expect everything to happen straight away. I didn't realise how slowly it was going to develop. We had been given information about certain things. We had to black out at night, not even a sliver of light must show; everyone had to put up some suitable window block to achieve this. If you needed to go outside during the hours of darkness you had to turn off the light before you opened the outer door. There were air raid wardens looking out for anyone transgressing. At a later stage most people fixed adhesive paper strips across their windows. This was to prevent any glass flying into the room if a bomb dropped nearby. There was a great air of uncertainty, expectancy and insecurity. Gradually it turned out that Hitler was quite happy to continue in Poland and leave us alone. We did, of course, go on preparing our war machine. We began to build new bombers and fighter aeroplanes, particularly the Hurricane and Spitfire fighters which were to be our shield in days to come, and the main bombers too – Wellingtons and Lancasters, particularly for long distance raids. Gradually we settled down to a steadier life. Although there were gaps in our expectations, we began to form a routine.

I persuaded father to build an air raid shelter on the nursery. I was afraid of glass splinters if a raid occurred. This we did, building quite a big one about twenty feet long by eight feet wide – brick lined and with a concrete top. I understand that quite a few people from nearby came up and used it when bombing did start. I was away in the Navy by that time. I made an error of judgement in getting father to have the tops cut off our exhibition chrysanthemums, which had almost reached bud stage. This we did and threw them away. When flowering time came round there was a shortage of chrysanthemum flowers for sale and they would have been quite valuable. I thought that the government would destroy all those types of plants. In fact we, as a specialist nursery were allowed to use a small space in our greenhouses to keep a few of each as stock so that after the war we could start again.

I remember, so well, feeling quite lost knowing that I would soon be called up for service. Nothing of the old life seemed to have any point. I just waited. Very soon everyone had an identity card, ration books came out for most food and gradually what were considered as luxuries began to disappear. Clothing was on ration. We were issued with coupons that represented so many points and everyone had to use points to buy clothes and clothing material. Gradually Xmas came and went with still no attack against us and we soldiered on.

In January 1940 I received my call-up papers. I had to attend a security office in Moor Street, Birmingham, to register. When I got there I was lined up with a crowd of other men and given a medical examination, which I passed, grade one. This I was pleased about as it allowed me to apply for and get into the Navy. They asked me what part of the forces I wanted to join. I said the Navy and if possible the medical service. Had I any qualifications for that? Yes, I had the various Red Cross certificates and some knowledge of X-rays. Good, go home and wait for my call up in three or four weeks. This I did and made preparations to meet the unknown.

A few weeks later, I received notification that I was to join the Navy and present myself to HMS Royal Arthur, in the middle of February, for initial training. HMS Royal Arthur was the Butlin's holiday camp at Skegness, which had been taken over by the Navy. I was glad the uncertainty was over. It's interesting that my father said, "I wish I was going instead of you." It is, as I found out, amazing how you become associated with and forever after have a soft spot for your service.

Chapter 2-

HMS ROYAL ARTHUR

The great day eventually arrived. My father took me in the car – petrol rationing hadn't really taken over by then. On the way there we stopped at a pub and had a good lunch. When I arrived at Royal Arthur and signed in, the first thing they offered me was a huge meal which I couldn't eat. In due course I was told to find chalet number so and so and wait to be called. I found there were to be three of us in three bunks. Unfortunately there was only one thin blanket each and it was not enough for March on the east coast of England.

I sat around in the hut, wanting to have a walk around but being afraid that they might call for me. Gradually the time went by and we went in for supper. There were still no further instructions so we returned to our hut and eventually went to bed. It was too cold to sleep properly and I really did miss home.

At 6 a.m. the next day there was a call to rise and shine over the loudspeakers. We were fetched outside and told to "Get fell-in." It was bitterly cold, snow showers were blowing in off the North Sea and we only had ordinary jackets and trousers. We had to wash in cold water and there was no heating in either the hut or bath hut.

After a bit of marching around we were sent in to breakfast. Food was plentiful, if a bit rough and I was still rather lost. I was due to stay at Royal Arthur for two weeks and then move on. We were allocated to classes, each class being under the charge of a Chief Petty Officer. We all sat in a room set out like a lecture room. The Chief introduced himself and said "You will, so long as you are here, address me as 'Sir'. You will be given instructions on the basics of marching and also begin to use naval terms. This is a ship and whether you are on a real ship or a shore station that remains so. You will be given your new kit of clothes and begin to feel that you are in the Navy. You will not be allowed out of the quarters for a week, after that you can go to Skegness about a mile away."

For organisational purposes we were divided into Watches, Red and Green that is Port and Starboard – Port being the left side of the ship and starboard the right side, when you are looking forward. Each watch was then divided into two parts. This meant that all the port watch was ashore (anywhere outside the Royal

Arthur) one night and all the starboard another. If conditions necessitated it only half of each watch could be out at any time and that meant you were ashore one night in four. It was impressed on us that leave was a privilege and no one was entitled to it. I felt at that time that it was a privilege to be alive and you must be careful. We learned that a floor was the deck, a wall was a bulkhead and a ceiling was a deckhead. We were given a number and told that we would remember it for the rest of our life. I didn't realise then just how right it was. Here I am sixty odd years later and I have no hesitation in recalling it, PMX 65063. P for Portsmouth, M for miscellaneous and X for hostilities only and had ceased to be Jack Woolman and had become Woolman PMX 65063 "SIR!" We were instructed that whenever you passed an Officer you saluted, not the snap up and down of the Army or Air Force but quietly lift your right arm up and place your hand just above your eyebrow.

Each morning the 0630 fall-in was repeated; each morning it was cold. One day we would have overcoats on, another we wouldn't. This did not seem to be related to the weather but whether or not someone had remembered to run a certain flag up. You had to check and go out accordingly.

We were taught the right way to lash up our hammock with the correct

At the "Royal Arthur" Skegness, 1940. Jack is 2nd from left in the back row.

number of lashings on it properly spaced out and were also issued with a suitcase and a small hand case. That was our kit and we were responsible for its cleanliness, tidiness and our general appearance. All our clothes were carried in the two cases and wherever we went they went with us. Often you had no other storage space and had to live directly out of your kit bag. Whatever you wanted always seemed to be at the bottom, which meant getting everything out. You also had to be fit and tidy enough for inspection at any time. Not easy.

One rather off-putting thing was that we were given our navy suit and cap. One morning we were told to go to the Quartermasters store and collect it. Unfortunately they didn't have enough of everything and all sizes. Nevertheless, they threw your things out through a hole in the wall (sorry, bulkhead) and you took it away. When you began to sort it out and put it on you found that you didn't necessarily have both a jacket and trousers and that whatever you did have didn't necessarily fit. It was quite amusing to see men walking around half civilian, half navy. This was the main reason they wouldn't let you go ashore for the first week. It was made quite clear that you had to go and swap your wrong clothes or fill the gaps yourself when the clothes were available. It gradually dawned on us that we were on our own now, no soft mother to ease our difficulties. I was lucky enough to get a reasonably well-fitting jacket, trousers and cap. Sadly there was no cap badge and I felt rather like a railway porter. In fact I seriously considered asking for a move to a different section, which I could have done.

I had to go home on my first leave with no cap badge and in a navy blue serge suit. I was still glad to go. It was whilst I was at Royal Arthur that I began smoking. On my first shore leave I went into Skegness with some pals, whom I now had to learn to call shipmates. We went into a tobacconist and bought some cigarettes and a cheap pipe. The latter was a horror until I eventually "burnt it in." It was like smoking cardboard with a general acrid nature.

I have often mused about the question of smoking. I spent much of my spare time with my cousin Gordon Osborne. When we were about five years old his mother let him smoke whenever he wanted to. My mother strongly opposed it and stopped me. As soon as I left the parental cocoon I began to smoke, Gordon never did after the first few tries.

The first time I had weekend leave I naturally went home. It meant going by train from Skegness to London and then on to Birmingham where father met me and took me home. Now rail travel wasn't, by then, as good as it used to be. For a start trains didn't run to time and you could never guarantee a seat. On this occasion I travelled for most of the journey sitting in the corridor on my suitcase.

I didn't mind. I was free. I would go anywhere once I'd managed to get out of those gates at Royal Arthur. That feeling never left me when I managed to go on shore leave either for a night or longer.

In due course, after a rather trying journey, I reached home. Although it wasn't a very generous leave – 7.00 a.m. on Saturday until 7.00 a.m. Monday morning – to me it was freedom. I was home again, once more being wrapped in cotton wool. We were all delighted to be a family again. I always felt that it was worse for my mother than for anyone else. Her first born, the apple of her eye, had been snatched away from her and no one would look after him, and he wasn't old enough to look after himself. (I was twenty!)

During the short time at home I saw as many of my friends as possible, feeling rather superior to them in as much as I was now a sailor in the Royal Navy. Never mind that I'd never been to sea.

Quickly the time passed and I had to go back. This meant catching a train at midnight on Sunday for London and hoping that I'd be able to get the connecting one to Skegness from Euston. This brought reality back into my world. However, I was lucky and successful, and a rather anxious and weary proto-sailor reached the Royal Arthur in good time.

This was before the war really began. There was no bombing and it was, although I didn't realise it, an easy journey. This I suppose was rather similar to what our instructor the Chief Petty Officer said "You lot don't realise how lucky you are to have someone as kind as I am who treats you gently." We laughed. Later we realised how true it was.

One item in our preliminary training was instruction relating to the use of gas masks. These were issued on the first day and we were told that we must carry them with us at all times. Anyone found without his mask would be punished. They were much bigger than the civilian ones for which they had been exchanged and were issued in a canvas haversack, which you slung over your shoulder. They didn't seem much different to those at home except that they were bigger and therefore more trouble. We didn't like carrying them but we were already being indoctrinated that when you were ordered to do something you unquestionably obeyed it. It wasn't your worry whether or not the order was right, wrong or even sensible!

Our attitude to gas masks changed when one day they took us to a hut with a door at each end. "Now" said the Chief, "You will put on your masks and go into this hut. You will walk through it and when you get to the other end you will take off your mask before you leave through the other door." We all put on our masks, walked one at a time through the door and along to the other end. The door was fastened. I took off my mask as instructed and was immediately assailed by gas. My eyes stung and watered. I began coughing heartily and was almost in a panic. Naturally I pushed against the door again and this time it came open and I exited as quickly as I could. "There" said the Chief, "Now you know what a gas mask is for – don't go out without it." From that time, I began to realise how the Navy instructed you by example. You only really understand what you have experienced.

We had an absorbing lecture on looking after yourself. What you should eat, drink and take care of. This was similarly rammed home by example. The Chief said above all look after your teeth. Don't neglect them and let toothache begin. "Look", he said, pointing out to sea. "You see that little ship out there? That's a minesweeper, with similar ratings on it to yourselves. It only comes into port every ten days. If one of them developed toothache he'd not be able to get any help until the next trip ashore." I never forgot that little homily. The rest of the lecture was about how to keep clean, look after your clothes etc., when you were in communal living conditions. You certainly needed a bit of encouragement to have a bath whilst at HMS Royal Arthur. The bath was in an unheated hut. It was early March and the wind was howling in from the North Sea. There was no hot water. I began to appreciate my previously comfortable life.

Whilst we were there we did a bit of rather untidy marching but they didn't worry too much as many of us were going into the miscellaneous sections such as medical and wouldn't really need the parade ground stuff.

Eventually the two weeks came to an end. Our kind Chief told us that it was usual to have a whip round for him before we left. This we cheerfully did, thinking that he was telling the truth and that it was one of the weird and wonderful ways of the Navy. He also told us that in two days we were going to the barracks at Portsmouth, HMS Victory. Then, because we were at the end of our course we were sent to pick up cigarette ends off the ground around the buildings. There weren't any, but that didn't matter. You must appear to be occupied. I met that on numerous occasions during my service.

Eventually Saturday, the wonderful day, came. I was naturally a bit excited about going to a real barracks, which again is a 'ship' called HMS Victory. At first the Navy's attitude to buildings, where all are called a ship and going into town is going ashore and all the rooms are cabins, seems a bit peculiar, but you soon see the sense of it and really feel you are on a ship. It certainly works.

We fell in on the parade ground at 0700 and were taken to Skegness Station by lorry, about one hundred of us. We had some breakfast before we left. We were going to London and then changing to our various ways. The train was half an hour late. This didn't please us but we just put up with it. In its own good time it arrived and we found that the rest of the journey had the same leisurely air about it. We just sat in the carriage and chatted or played cards.

In time, it became apparent that no one had thought to arrange any food for us. I managed to buy a bun at one of the stations. You didn't know quite what to do. The train had stopped at the station but no one had any idea for how long. On the platform, a little way along was a trolley selling tea and buns. Did you risk missing the train by getting out and buying some, or stay on it and remain hungry? In the end I risked it. I suppose this was what people meant when they said the Navy made you independent. In other words you often didn't know what you were supposed to do. You had to decide for yourself.

Gradually we made our way towards London and then over to Portsmouth. We arrived there at about 8 o'clock in the evening or, as I should say 2000 hrs, and hung around on the platform for half an hour. It transpired that we hadn't got a lorry to take us to barracks because we were so late. They decided to march us to HMS Victory carrying our own kit i.e. a suitcase and small case and hammock. This wouldn't have been so bad had I not developed a real 'flu cold a couple of days before and I truly felt like passing out. We eventually staggered into barracks. At the gate we were issued with a card, which proved that we were there and that I was in port watch second part. This would allow me to go ashore every fourth evening and back by 2300. We were also informed where we should live. The barracks consisted of a number of large oblong blocks four storeys high. I was in D4. With a big effort I staggered over to block D and then had to carry my kit and myself up to the top floor. Ready to collapse I checked that I was in the right place and to my horror found I was in C4. Down I went, kit and all, to the next door block and once again up to its top floor. I could hardly see. The situation in which I found myself wasn't exactly encouraging. A long room had a row of lockers down the middle and hooks for hammocks on the sidewall and middle of the room supports. It was getting late and besides I was exhausted, tired and hungry not having had anything except that railway wartime bun since half past six that morning. I needed to, as they say, get my head down (up in a hammock in fact), but where? The room was quite large with maybe one hundred hammock hooks in it, but half of them were already occupied with men asleep and the rest all had bits of paper on the hooks with a number on. They were obviously intended to be reserved for men who were ashore for the evening and even though it was unofficial I knew it would have considerable force on their return. Where to sling my hammock was the question. I, a sailor of a fortnight didn't fancy my chance against an old salt! Just down the room was a man in his hammock who was not asleep. I went down to him. "Excuse me," I said. He looked at me and weighed me up as a freshman. "Can you tell me where I can sling my hammock please?" He thought for a bit and said "Buggered if I know" in the helpful way that the Navy had when you ask a silly question. What was my next move? I didn't fancy slinging my hammock and being turned out when it's owner returned, probably irate and somewhat drunk too.

By then I was tired out and desperate so I removed one of the labels and slung my hammock. I didn't make much of a job of it, as it was the first time I'd used it, but I managed. I didn't have a stretcher to make it more comfortable. A stretcher is a length of wood about eighteen inches long which you put across the end of your hammock just above your pillow. This prevents your hammock sides from falling in over your face, which is unpleasant. I didn't sleep very well but at least I could lie down and rest. No one came to claim the hooks, which was a relief. About 0630 I was wakened by men getting up and dressed and by the loud speakers giving out information and orders. Along the middle of the deck was a row of tabling where we ate meals. Since the hammocks were slung up and across the table anyone getting out of the hammock put their feet on the table and then climbed off. It was the first time I'd had breakfast with bare, or semi-bare, bodies landing at intervals amongst my utensils.

Chapter 3

HMS VICTORY &
TRAINING AT HASLAR

We had become used to the Royal Arthur and felt more comfortable there. Moving to the Victory meant that I had to begin all over again to do what we called "making your corner." It meant that you learned as quickly as possible what you could get away with to make yourself comfortable where you lived - not easy, but necessary. Next morning we were up, fed, washed and shaved by 0700 and "fell-in" on the parade ground which was the area all across the centre with barrack blocks all the way round. This was called the quarterdeck and you had to cross it "at the double" which meant you had to run, even if you were carrying something. This applied to all navy ships.

We had a bit of marching and then were put in a small room, which was a first aid station. During our duty hours this was where we had to be. There was nothing to do but we were supposed to keep busy. Every so often an Officer on "rounds" would poke his head in and say something like "is everything correct?" The senior rating would say it was and he'd go away. The snag was that although we were in there most of the day and were supposed to be keeping the place clean there was nothing to keep six ratings occupied, but you mustn't be caught doing nothing. The solution we worked out was to bring in a book and read it behind our open small case, keeping a duster in our hand. If the Officer came in we just shut the book into the case and buffed something with the duster.

On one occasion we were told to go to the clothing store and collect our number six trousers, which we did. When we got there they measured us in all the places that tailors do and slung us a pair of white duck trousers though the window. When we had a chance to have a look at them later we found that they were all the same size! Suits were numbered according to their purpose. A best suit, which was called a doeskin, a rather smart cloth, the name being descriptive, was the number one. The working suit was number three etc. Number ones had gold stripes and badges and number three's had red ones. That is when you'd been in long enough to get them. In the navy stripes indicate service, one for three years, two for five years, and five for seven years. There is, sewn on above them your rate. One anchor is for a leading hand and two crossed anchors for Petty Officer. If you reached the exalted rank of Chief Petty Officer you lost all your sleeve badges and had a row of ball-like buttons round the end of your sleeve.

After a few days of losing ourselves we were mustered on the quarterdeck, marched into a lorry and transported over the harbour to Haslar Hospital. This was to be my resting place for a year or two. Once again I was given a duty card with my off-duty times, that is my watch, port or starboard etc.

The staff quarters were situated in a brick building well away from the hospital which was a large four floor building in the centre of the grounds. The top room was the sleeping quarters and the ground floor the living quarters. I was one of about one hundred men in the sleeping quarters. Once again we had hammock hooks so that you could sling it across the room but this time there was no central table. We had the usual metal locker for our clothes and our kitbag, which stood along side it on the floor. It was locked by an ingenious piece of apparatus that was threaded through the holes at the top and was then secured by a padlock. You have to look after your valuables carefully, if you didn't no one else would. In charge was a Chief Petty Officer who was sharp, acid and fussy. If you hadn't done your hammock properly you were called back. If you left anything out of its correct place, you were reprimanded. If you weren't smart and clean, you were reprimanded. We were reminded of the instructor at Royal Arthur telling us how gently we were being treated. He was right; this was quite different.

The messing, that is the supply and serving of food was arranged as follows. There was a galley occupied by a "cook of the mess" who was appointed to purchase and serve the food after it had been cooked by the main galley. It was a system that benefited the cook rather than the eater! On the morning after we arrived we were directed to a classroom where we were to spend twelve weeks being taught about medicine and nursing. In peacetime it used to be twelve months, but there wasn't the time to spare, so it was concentrated.

The first part of our stay at Haslar coincided with the phoney war. The Germans were concentrating on Poland; and later Belgium, Holland, Czechoslovakia and ultimately France. There was no fighting war as far as we were concerned. The only signs of war that we saw were a few scouting planes at night. They used to fly at a considerable height and you watched them being traced by the searchlights until eventually they were caught. They looked like a moth in a candle. The anti aircraft guns used to fire regularly at them, but I never saw one hit.

Life went on uneventfully, I enjoyed the instruction we were having. We eventually had enough knowledge to be able to handle anything that happened from a first aid point of view. This was because if you were drafted to a small ship you might not have a doctor (always called a "quack") on board, and had to be able to deal with whatever happened yourself. (We were always known as "Doc"). Eventually Hitler turned his efforts on us, and life was in a different world.

We were on a routine that began at 0730 the next morning. If we went ashore we had to be back at the hospital either by midnight or 1100 the next morning. When we went ashore we often used to stay the night in Portsmouth at one of the sailor's clubs such as those run by the YMCA, Salvation Army or Aggie Westons, a historic well-known dormitory where you could always get a cheap meal. You paid around two shillings (ten pence) for the meal, usually baked beans, bacon and sausage. The night's sleep cost you about five shillings (twenty five pence) but it wasn't quite what you would think. The various clubs had a number of beds set in cubicles and you could always book those if there were any available. If there weren't you had to sleep in the extra rooms they had taken over for the war. If you paid in advance during the afternoon it was reserved for you. If not you could drop in when you were ready to go to bed and see if there were any spaces left. The sleeping quarters consisted of several rooms with nothing in them except mattresses on the floor. There was just enough room between them to have access. There were perhaps twenty or more in a room and that was were you slept; if you were able to. When you think that the windows were all blacked out and boarded up it was quite a shock to open the door and go in around midnight. You didn't normally undress, just took of your jacket and trousers, put your money under your pillow for security and made the best of it. By morning the air was thick and you were glad to get away. It had, perhaps, enabled you to go to a dance and then get back to quarters the next morning, so it was worth tolerating the conditions.

Another development that helped life to be a bit more civilised was that I found I could have petrol coupons for a weekend leave, instead of rail passes. I brought my car down from home, garaged it in Portsmouth and used it as far as petrol allowed. The garage was on the waterfront behind a public house, just opposite to the harbour station. This was fine when I just went to Haslar. When the bombing began though I felt that I'd lose my car quite quickly, so I moved it to another garage at Brockenhurst, a few miles out on the Gosport side. Later in the war they dropped a bomb nearby and I almost lost it there. The irony was that the original garage was still intact at the end of the war. It was almost the only building left standing in that area.

Soon after we had settled in, we began our training. It was virtually going to school again. We all sat at desks in rows, the instructor standing in front of his blackboard. The main difference was that we were in the Navy and were subject to naval discipline. We began to absorb navy life. We had to learn anatomy and physiology, plus general first aid treatment for common illnesses. The training for sick berth staff, as they were called, had to be a bit over that of ordinary nurses because some would be sent to small ships without a doctor and you had to be able to cope. I soon learned that the "Docs" were treated with sympathy by other branches for two reasons. They never knew when they might have to inject them for something and we had to give them a condom if they asked for one when they were going ashore. The later stages of our training included a few hours a week on a ward, just to get the idea of it.

This leads me to an incident in May 1940. I was home on a short weekend leave, which meant that I had to be back at the hospital by midnight on Sunday. I drove back in my car on Sunday evening and when I was within about twenty miles of Portsmouth an increasing number of vehicles, buses and similar came past me from the direction of the coast. They were full of soldiers. Wondering what was happening I reached the hospital at Haslar expecting to go to my quarters as usual. Not so, however. On reporting to the Duty Officer as I came in I was told to get ready and go up to one of the top wards, on duty for the evening. Usually empty for emergency use, they were now full of soldiers just arrived back from Dunkirk.

Hitler had quickly overrun France and had almost encircled our forces who had fought a wonderful retreat back to the sea at Dunkirk. This was the occasion of Churchill's "little boats" affair. He, on being told that thousands of our men had been driven back to the sea ordered a call for help from all the privately owned boats in Britain. Everything from river cruisers to small craft answered the call and they were sent over. The idea was that they could get close in to shore to pick up the men whilst being given covering fire by our Royal Navy ships, to which they transferred them. It was a terrible experience, our men having been pinned down by German land and air forces for many days with no adequate food or cover. They had fought back from the Maginot Line area and then had to stay on the beaches under constant fire for days.

These were some of the men whom I found when I reported to my ward. The lads I came across were amongst those not wounded physically but very shocked and in a pretty poor general condition. There was no counselling in those days, everyone was supposed to just get over it and get back on duty.

The ward was under the charge of an LSBA (Leading Sick Berth Attendant), and there was just me to help him. I had finished half my training by then and a ward was still a strange place to me. Most of our patients were not wounded but just exhausted. They had been on the beach for many days; some without proper food. Some had not had their bowels moved for a week or more. The LSBA came up to me and said, "Give this man an enema." I had been taught in training what to do. How different it is when theory becomes reality!

If I pushed a tube into him should I hurt or damage him? How hot was comfortably hot? How big was a piece of soap as big as a walnut? All these things pass quickly through your mind. I think the real problem is that, when it comes to the crunch, if you do hurt someone it is done and cannot be undone. I went to the LSBA. "What do I do for the enema?" I asked. "Bloody hell" he said, "Don't they teach you anything nowadays?" He told me in no uncertain terms! Actually I knew but was afraid, due to my lack of experience.

The training was coming to an end. We had been through as much of the basics as could be pushed into twelve weeks. Actually we had been taught very thoroughly. We were not left with any lack of theory and only experience could give us the rest of the training. We had to learn about the physical aspects of the body and as much about illnesses and injuries as we could. If you were drafted on to a small ship such as a minesweeper and something happened – anything from a toothache to a leg blown off you had to be able to deal with it until full treatment was possible. Part of the training was simple learning and up to the individual, but the Navy had some excellent mnemonics e.g. "Silly sailors can't piss therefore tons (of) muddy urine" helped us to learn the names of the bones in the hand (Scaphoid, Semilunar, Cuneiform, Pisiform, Trapezium, Trapezoid, Magnum, Unciform).

The instruction reached its conclusion and exams became the worry. A doctor who was also a pharmacist carried out the pharmacy tests. Now we hadn't been taught any pharmacy because at Sick Berth Attendant level we were not likely to be expected to use it. Before the end of the course rumours began that to pass that section we didn't have an exam. All we had to do was take the examiner a tin of navy-issue tobacco and he would pass us. This developed into a practical certainty and we all armed ourselves with the necessary. On the morning of the exam, over we went to the pharmacy. The medical teaching we had received was tested in sections, anatomy, physiology, treatment etc. and was thorough and excellent. Then we came to the pharmacy. It was very simple and both the examiner and the trainees knew the position. He asked us all two questions, one of which was name two disinfectants; the other was just as simple. My answer was Dettol and TCP. Having a bit of fun with me and thinking I should be stumped he said, "What do the letters stand for?" I said trichloro phenyl methyl iodosalicyl". This completely amazed him. When the exam results were announced for pharmacy he gave all the others a pass and gave me a pass superior! It just shows you what a bit of cheek will do. You learn all the while you are in the service never to say, "I can't do something." Just do as you are told and keep your fingers crossed. The pass meant that I was now SBA Sick Berth Attendant instead of a PSBA (Provisional Sick Berth Attendant) and my pay was increased. I now received fourteen shillings per week (seventy pence) but I must pay half to my next of kin. Jolly days!

Chapter 4-

HASLAR AS A QUALIFIED SBA

The first change that resulted from my passing out was starting full time on a ward. I was put on the acute surgical, which dealt primarily with injuries from accidents and enemy action. I remember vividly one sailor who had his leg amputated after a fight between a British and German STB (lightly armed speed boat) had badly injured it. He frequently complained about pain from his leg and often it was bad enough to make him yell. It was the one that had been cut off at the top of the thigh. His nerves told him that it was still there.

At that time we were also doing a lot of work on burns. Damage of this kind was frequent and disabling. The problem was scar tissue forming in the damaged areas after they healed. There were also many patients in with more mundane problems, such as ruptures. It meant that sooner or later I had to take someone down to the operating theatre and remain there whilst they were being operated on. The first time you felt a mixture of fearfulness, excitement and anxiety. However you soon became accustomed to it and it became interesting. I always felt better when the first cut through the skin had taken place. Working inside an opened body wasn't so disturbing somehow.

Ordinary day duties were interesting and there was plenty to learn. I was just about the lowest official grade in the ward, of course. The rest of the staff consisted of leading hands, known as Killicks, VAD nurses who had joined for the war period, and SBA's such as myself, who did anything from cleaning urine bottles to taking people down to the operating theatre. In charge was either a Killick or a Petty Officer (the next rating up) together with a Ward Sister. Theoretically the Sick Berth staff were in charge of the navy side of the organisation and the Sister responsible for the nursing side. In fact it was a matter of working together. The hours of duty were not bad, unless there was an emergency. We started a full duty day at 0745 and finished at 2045 with time off for meals. Every other day was a leave day when we finished at 1300. We were then able to go ashore, which meant into Gosport or Portsmouth. We were, of course, still on the naval system of Port (red) and Starboard (green) watches. Besides our shore leave we were allowed every other week, alternately a short or a long weekend. Long was 0800 on Saturday to 1200 on Monday. Short leave was the same start but returning by midnight on Sunday. These allowed us to go home if we wished. That was where my car came in.

We were now entering the lead-up to the Battle of Britain. We had been kicked out of Europe when Dunkirk ended our efforts and left us on our own to try to survive. I well remember the saying amongst us. "Oh well we'll be alright because we're playing at home now." I can recall the feeling of surprise that in only a few months Poland Holland, Belgium, and even France had been annihilated by the German force. None of us had any previous idea of their strength, and none of us had the slightest doubt that we would win in the end. It was a good job we didn't known the true position, perhaps! There were two occasions when I was delighted with the news. The first was when Hitler attacked Russia and the other when America came in. Each time, when I woke up in the morning and heard the news I said, "Thank God for that." I knew that we would be all right. Hitler had set out his plans, he had conquered and held the continent and held the Mediterranean. After the defeat of France he tried to make peace with us but I am sure that his intention was to keep us quiet whilst he beat the Russians and recovered, then told us what to do and eventually either took us over or controlled us. Various plans were discovered telling how he would treat the British and they all followed the plans he used for Poland, and the other countries. Firstly wipe out the Jews and then destroy the country itself. It seemed a terrific job, which was why many people thought he was bluffing. He almost succeeded. If we had not kept our faith and continued to resist him he would have done it.

We were now in mid 1940. I had passed my exams and was finding my feet working on the ward. There was, just then, a problem with patients and air raids. At that early stage, when the Battle of Britain was just developing, the routine was to get them ready when the yellow warning was put through and to take them down on the red warning. When it reverted to yellow, we took them up again. This was fine so long as there wasn't another yellow (which meant that they were coming in our direction) when we had to take them down again. As the raids began to increase it was a terrific upset when all the patients who could be moved were and it often happened several times per night. Someone had the bright idea of having another warning – purple. This meant we moved them down on yellow, stayed down until a purple was called and then bought them back. If it changed to yellow, we took them down again. On bad nights some patients being carried on stretchers were no sooner on their way down than they were coming up again. They moved down and up so often that some of them were half way down the stairs all night, neither one thing nor the other. It was finally decided to take them down in the early evening and leave them there all night. There were some who were not well enough to be moved, even on a stretcher. They had to stay in the ward and hope for the best. We staff were instructed to stay with them and take our chance. There were several nights when we took shelter under a bed. On one occasion I saw a Sister under a bed and a patient comforting her. On another occasion I listened to a Churchill speech whilst I was sheltering. They were wonderful speeches. Everyone looked forward to them. On the occasion mentioned it was the one that said, "Hitler says he is going to wring our necks like a chicken. Some chicken, some neck!" The way he said it brought a flood of hope to us all. I doubt if we'd have won the war without him.

The early stage of the air fight was developing. The Luftwaffe was seriously attacking the fighter stations all along the south coast, shooting down our planes in comfort and bombing the airfields mercilessly. The plan was to shoot our air force out of the sky and then invade us. We used to stand and watch the vapour trail patterns that each plane made, high above us in the sky, loops of white, like smoke. We also had to fight off the bombers that were coming in to attack the airfields. We were greatly helped by the new development of what we called radio direction finding (RDF). The Americans called it radar and that was that term which we eventually adopted. A number of radio masts were placed round the coasts and beams were sent out. These bounced back off the planes and left a pattern on the screen at the receiving centres. This enabled us to keep a maximum number of planes in reserve and send the others out to the exact area where they were needed. There were also many centres where human observers were operating and passing messages on to HQ.

The Battle of Britain began in the early summer of 1940 and gradually increased in activity until the autumn. During the summer, at the height of the attack, when planes either bombed Portsmouth and Southampton or passed us by on their way to towns further north, we were sent down the cellars with the patients at dusk. We were also allocated fire-watching duties. This meant going up in the roof of the hospital to report and if possible deal with any fire bombs that were dropped. We weren't told how to deal with high explosive bombs! There were several incidents that I remember in detail still.

One night there was a particularly heavy attack on Portsmouth and I was on middle watch, which was midnight to 0400 hours. Slowly the time crept round to my watch and at about a quarter to midnight I started my journey into hell. That is no exaggeration. The night was full of high explosive bombs, firebombs, gunfire, machines flying over and around, searchlights trying to find them and the general noise from fires and fighting. The hospital was about four stories high. I went up slowly, at every step the noise and apparent danger increased. On reaching the first floor I began to be truly frightened. At the second I began to wait and at the third I honestly didn't feel I dared go any further. It seemed like committing suicide. I stopped and considered the position -Not logically; it wasn't a time for logic, just a confusion of thought and fear for my life. At one point I realised that if I didn't go on I'd be in serious trouble. I was in serious trouble anyway so that didn't weigh too heavily. In my jumble of thoughts and feelings it occurred to me that if I didn't go up and take over from one of my mates, he would have to stay there. It was a difficult decision but it was, as I've already said, a time when feelings took over from logic. I had to go up and I did. On the roof was a scared SBA who couldn't get away down quickly enough. I looked around me and it was all lit up by fires. You could hear the swish of baskets of firebombs, high explosives and gunfire in a cacophony of noise. There seemed to be nowhere to hide. I just crouched up there, behind the brickwork around the roof, occasionally taking a look over and around. There were tracer bullets from both guns on the ground and planes. Occasionally a plane was shot down; not many though and of course it didn't help whoever or whatever it finally fell on. Very slowly the time moved on, the bombing and attack eased until it had, with a final isolated bomb, finished. At 0400 hours my relief came up and I went down, confused by fear but thankful that I had carried out my duty. One of the benefits of going through the war was that I learned that if I had to do something that I was afraid of, I could make myself do it. This gives you confidence and I believe I can still do the same, even now.

Life had to go on. In the morning we started again in the hospital. There was a lot of damage, in fact the very wall that I had run alongside to get from staff quarters to the cellars was down. That must have been the big bang that occurred just after I reached those cellars. More luck for Jack. Had I not had several such fortunate turns I would not be writing this now.

There was another incident soon after, which at the time we thought was very amusing. The hospital was supplied with water via one of those old-fashioned water tanks made from metal squares and standing quite high in the air. When the Battle of Britain began, a space at the top was metal lined and made into an observation post. One of the sick berth staff was posted up there on watches all day to ring down to ARP control in the hospital cellar. All went well for a while until a rating named Smith was on duty one day. About mid day there was a frantic call from the tower. "Warning, warning, hair raid here, with hair craft hover the hisland (Isle of Wight) thousands of 'em, hi'm hoff" and he came down. Forever afterwards he was known as henemy haircraft Smith. I must admit I couldn't blame him. I'd been up there myself and you felt as if you'd be the first and obvious target.

We became so used to the daily raids with hundreds of aircraft overhead making the famous vapour trails that we mostly were interested in how our side was doing. Every night we used to listen to the score on the radio when we were told the number of German planes shot down, and the British planes lost. We had to deduct some of our successes and increase the number of our losses to bring it somewhere about right. The two countries were always biased towards their side. The losses of German planes crept up each day during August and September 1940. When the one great day came we were sure that the activity had been very heavy, from the mass of vapour trails we could see, and when it was announced that night that we had shot down a record number of German planes we were all very cheered.

This was the time when Hitler decided that he couldn't sustain his great losses, and he turned his efforts from bombing the airfields to night bombing. This was one of the decisions that ultimately lost him the war. Our numerically inadequate air force was just getting towards defeat; airstrips and air stations

Food and drink set out on table at Haslar, Xmas 1941.

were being blown up before they could be repaired. The truly wonderful RAF men were becoming exhausted and supplies of planes were barely keeping up with losses. A little while longer and we'd have been faced with defeat. This would have given Hitler air control and he would have invaded.

There were one or two personal experiences that have remained in my mind all these years. The first was during the heavy raids. One day we went on shore leave to Portsmouth. This meant crossing the harbour from Gosport to Pompey by ferry. The boat was, as usual, fairly full and we went astern to get away from the jetty. During this, the propeller made a swishing noise. It sounded just like the noise that a basket of firebombs made when they were dropping near to you. All the people in the boat, including me, dropped flat on our faces, an automatic reaction that illustrates the effect the daily raids had on all of us.

On another occasion I was going over on the ferry when an air raid siren sounded just as we were half way across. On reaching shore we were sent into a brick air raid shelter on the quayside. I went in and as I did so glanced back and saw coming in across the harbour, quite low, about fifty German planes. My immediate reaction was if they are coming to bomb the harbour I am in it and I've had it. The brick air raid shelter certainly would not have protected us from any near misses let alone a direct hit. The next few minutes were anxious ones but the planes, to my amazement, went right over us and did not drop any bombs. This was explained later when we heard that they were the fighter escort for a number of bombers. Our fighters had been sent to attack them and had successfully split the fighters from the bombers. We had seen the fighters. The bombers had diverted to Southampton. Life was on a slender thread in those days.

I was walking back one night from a dance in Southsea to my bed at Aggie Westons home. There was only a light bombing raid that evening but there were still a few planes buzzing around up above. Suddenly out of a front door of one of the houses dashed an old man, followed by his wife. "Can you help us please, we've got a fire bomb in our roof.?" Just at that moment I'd rather have gone on to my bed than take on a job like that, but what choice have you? I asked them if they had a stirrup pump, a water sprayer that was widely used for the purpose. "No" they said, "All we've got is that sand bag," pointing to one outside the front door. I thought I might just as well get on with it whilst I still could. They took me upstairs onto the landing and pointed to a three-foot square trap in the ceiling. "It's up there." "Have you got a ladder?" I asked. "No, but we've got a pair of steps." When they brought them they were not high enough. However by standing on the top I could just reach the ceiling and after putting up the sand bag, pulled myself up until I could peer over the edge of the trap door. The whole roof was full of flame and smoke. Right at the opposite end of the space was a bomb spluttering away where the roof met the wall. I heaved myself up into the roof space and surveyed the situation. I had to walk along the beams, which held up the ceiling of the room below, and try to get to and deal with the bomb. One rather disturbing thought crossed my mind. We had recently been told that when dealing with a fire bomb beware, because they were now being mixed with high explosive to make it harder to deal with them. We were recommended to hold a sand bag in front of our face for protection. I set out across the beam with the sand bag in the advised position, the nearer to the firebomb the worse it seemed. It was giving off flames, and lighting everything up like we had been told hell would be. There were clouds of unpleasant smoke lit by a red glow. As I was slowly edging my way along the beam, sand bag in front of my face, I suddenly thought they had not told me how to protect the rest of my body! Eventually I reached the bomb, the core of which appeared to be about the size of an orange and I realised how ill equipped I was to deal with it. All I had was the sandbag. The only thing I could think of was to try to smother it with sand. I dropped the bag on the bomb and it disappeared. "Oh hell, it has burned through the ceiling!" I thought. "Now it will set the rest of the house on fire." Just then the old lady called up, "It's OK it has fallen into the bath" which was, according to regulations, kept half full of water to help the householder deal with a fire. I had succeeded. The bomb was out, the old folk were happy and I was thankful. As I clambered out of the roof and down the stairs they thanked me profusely. I said without thinking "That's all right, any time!"

There were many such incidents happening all over the country and most people had their "bomb" story to tell. I remember one night when a raid was on and I was caught on the way back to Haslar at about 10pm. It was not a particularly heavy raid but there was a teenage girl in the shelter just on the Portsmouth side of Haslar creek and she was terrified. I spent the next half hour with my arms around her talking to her to calm her down. When the air raid ended I made my way back to Haslar and never met her again. It was a time of fleeting moments, which often included matters of life and death but very quickly moved on.

Things also moved on at the hospital. One day I saw a notice that asked for anyone with a working knowledge of photography to report to the office. I was tempted to go straight away, but I had already learned caution. They might want to put me on the front of a landing craft with a camera! Eventually I managed to find out that they needed a clinical photographer at the hospital. Having no knowledge of that particular specialisation I boldly marched in to see the

Warrant Officer in charge. "I've come to see about the request for a photographer, Sir." (Everything was a request in those days. If you wanted to grow a beard you put in a request to cease shaving. If it was granted it had to remain in force for six months!)

I was welcomed with open arms. I was told to bring back a sample of my work when I went home on my next weekend leave. This I did and took it in to show him on my return. All went well and I was accepted and told to report to the X-ray dept. to the Chief who was doing the clinical job at present, but wasn't good enough.

I soon found out that there were four staff there. The Chief, who wasn't on X-ray duty, a Petty Officer in charge, a leading hand and a couple of SBA's learning X-ray. The Chief didn't exactly welcome me with enthusiasm but I didn't expect him to anyway. The first thing I found out was he didn't want me to take any photos or do any processing. The outcome was that for about two months I simply sat in the darkroom twiddling my thumbs whilst he tried to have me taken away. This was because he was a retired Chief who had been brought back for the war. He had found a soft number and was going to hang on to it. I found out from the X-ray lads that he had already had three applicants taken away by tricking them into making mistakes. I had learned by then that in the Navy the Lord helps those who help themselves. So I decided to do exactly what he told me. At least he couldn't then report that I wasn't suitable. After a couple of months (sixty percent of the time in the darkroom) two jobs came along which were urgent. He reluctantly gave me one of them to do. We were at that time experimenting with the treatment of burns, which were an important cause of disability. I had never used photoflood lights before and I knew that I had to make a success of this or he would have had me out. I decided that if I set the lights equally I could not go far wrong. I took the pictures using a Kodak clinical camera, a real beauty for the job and took them to our own little darkroom for processing. The camera used eight inch x six inch size cut film, in dark slides which held the film. There were two films in each slide, which slid into the holder one on each side. To enable you to know which was already exposed, one side of the cover was black and the other was silver, you turned them over accordingly. Since by then it was time for dinner I went off to the staff quarters leaving the slides, four exposed and two not. When I came back from my meal I was about to take out the film and process it when I noticed that all the dark slides were showing the silver unexposed side. I knew that I had left them four and two, that meant that I didn't know which holders were exposed and which not. It also meant that someone had been into our locked darkroom and had tampered with them. The only two people with a key were myself, and the Chief. I developed all six of the films and thus averted what I am sure would have been goodbye to me. His purpose was that he could have said that I wasn't capable and that I'd missed an unrepeatable photograph in a series for burns treatment. I would have gone and he would have stayed, in what was a soft number not to mention a fascinating one. He, of course, said nothing, and neither did I.

A few days later as I was walking across the hospital to the X-ray department, I came up with the Warrant Officer. As we passed he said, "Ah, Woolman." "Yes sir?" "How are you getting on with the photo job?" "Fine, thank you sir" "Can you do it on your own?" "Yes sir." "Good," and he walked on. I knew basically what he meant and went on my way. Nothing changed for a week and then one morning when I went on duty the Chief was in there. As soon as I opened the door I was greeted with a tirade of naval oaths that aren't repeatable in print. Ending with, "I've got a draft to Scapa Flow and it's your sodding fault." With that he stormed out never to be seen again; so far as I was concerned. The X-ray lads were delighted. He had been so unpopular they were glad that someone had beaten him at his own game. This for me was the start of about twelve months of great interest and learning.

Chapter 5-

HASLAR AFTER THE CHIEF IN THE PHOTOGRAPHY DEPARTMENT LEFT

My job meant taking pictures of anything to do with injury or illness, when a record was needed, so that more could be taken later for comparison. I was officially attached to the X-ray dept. but had my own darkroom, quite small, at the top of the building. In it was a bench on which was an old enlarger with a horizontal throw instead of the modern vertical ones. You don't need much throw to enlarge from eight inches x six inches to ten inches x eight inches! The usual shots were in black and white orthochromatic film. This was better than the now popular panchromatic for that type of photo, especially where you needed to show up lesions on the skin, as the contrast was greater. On one occasion I was asked to copy a colour picture from a book for the medical specialist. In those days colour was very poor and not often used. I had never processed it before and so I was a bit doubtful about my ability. I had already found, though, that if an Officer, especially, in this case, a Rear Admiral, said he wanted something done you just said "Yes sir!" even if you didn't know how to do it. You jolly well found out. Only the word used should not be jolly! This I successfully did and my marks went up a bit. It was, in fact, a matter of pride that a number of my photos were used to illustrate articles in periodicals such as the British Medical Journal.

In the spring of 1942 we were told that there was to be a visit by King George VIth and Queen Elizabeth (now the Queen Mother). Even in wartime there was a flutter in the dovecotes. Everyone was to be included. When I heard that the hospital staff were to form a guard of honour along the footpath that their route followed and that we would be likely to be standing outside for about two hours, I wasn't so keen. I decided that I had better ask to become the official photographer for the occasion. This was granted, giving me the freedom to roam wherever I wished. Later I was restricted by the injunction that I must not be visible to the official party as they walked around. This limited me considerably and, after looking around, I decided that I'd have to use suitable windows on the first floor. Although I had a good, clear view, I was quite a way away from the visitors as they walked round. I was using my own camera, a Zeiss Nettar, which took roll film, but I had no telephoto facility. Added to this it was a dull, sunless day and it left little room for mistakes. In the event, all went well and I did a roaring trade afterwards from the Officers and Sisters involved.

Another break from routine was an outside session at Whale Island, nearby. There was much concern about sailors being hurt by explosions such as depth charges when a submarine was attacked after it had sunk a ship, leaving many men in the water. The experiment that I was to photograph, was to put a number of sheep in the water carefully spaced out by being tethered to ropes. When post mortems were carried out afterwards we knew exactly how far each unfortunate sheep had been from the explosive. For these outside photos taken from a small launch, I used my own 35mm camera. The explosions were set off, the sheep

Visit of King George VI & Queen Elizabeth (now Queen Mother), Spring 1942.

were taken and killed and I had to photograph any bits and pieces that had been damaged by the explosion pressurising the water, particularly of their lungs as they were affected the most. My job also meant going to the operating theatre for record photos and occasionally a post mortem. It was a fascinating and varied job.

I mentioned the Rear Admiral. There were two of them at Haslar then, one medical and the other surgical. They were the two top specialists who had been brought in from 'Civvy Street' just for the war and were very pleasant men. I also had to work for a Commander who was regular Navy and 'knew his place!' I was, however, able to keep him quiet because I always had a bit of work to finish for the Admiral. If he came along and wanted a job done at the double quick time I used to tell him that I would do my very best but I had to finish a job first for the Admiral. He knew that although they were H.O. (hostilities only) they were, for the time, Admirals and 'he knew his place!'

The one bonus was that I was whilst on that job I was "stopped draft". The admiral and others said they needed me to stay to do the job. I knew that eventually this would come to an end but just kept my fingers crossed. One day it did. The Commander told me that I had been put on draft but he said that first he needed to find a replacement. I must be aware that this was happening. The immediate difference was that I was put back on ward duty.

Soon after, I went sick with tonsilitis. When I came back to duty they said, "You're a lucky so & so, you've missed a draft to Russian convoys whilst you were sick." The position at that time was that we were losing about three quarters of our ships in the convoy and I honestly don't think I should have been here today had I not gone sick. Good old tonsillitis! Soon after that I was told that I had a draft to HMHS Tjitjalengka a hospital ship of 10,972 tons, and that I was to report to HMS Victory, the Portsmouth barracks. Changes like that are always unsettling. You have to find your way around again. After you have been on a ship for a while you find out where there is a quiet spot or where you can get a supply of milk, tea and sugar for an off-duty cup of tea, or 'char' as it was usually known. This is known as 'making a corner for yourself.'

A few months before this I met a girl who was to be my future wife, although we didn't know it then. One afternoon my shipmates and I decided we would go to a dance in Southsea when we went ashore that evening. We used to do this occasionally and ignored any bombing raids. In the early days of air raids all the places of entertainment had to close down in the evening in case a direct hit on a place such as a cinema caused unbearable casualties. It wasn't long before the public became bored with no entertainment and they were allowed to open again, slowly at first, up to about 8 o'clock and then later. When evening came one or two of the group decided that, as there was a dance in the hospital that night (they used to be held about once a month), we may as well go there. I strongly resisted the idea as when I had been to one before I didn't find it any fun. It was just sick berth staff and VAD nurses who worked there. However the majority supported the hospital dance and that was where we went. During the evening I met a nurse and danced with her. We enjoyed each other's company and agreed to meet again, which we did. In fact we became a regular pair. It was a bit difficult to get the same shore leave but working in the same place helped us. We had only been together for about three months when Enid was drafted to Cullercoats to work at the naval base there. We were almost restricted to contact by letter only. We did however managed to get a few leaves that coincided and either we went to her home for a short time or later we went to mine. It was wartime and you had to do the best you could and there was no point in grumbling.

Life went on much as before. One job has particularly stayed in my mind. I was told there would be an operation next morning where I had to take some photographs for record purposes. I remember thinking about the problems of a steamed-up lens if you went from cool to warm and so I went down to the theatre and left my camera there in good time to warm up. Before the time the operation was due to start I went and checked and all was well, the lens was clear. I kept my head down whilst they prepared themselves. The patient was wheeled in, put on the table and away it went. In due course they were ready for me to take the shot. In this case it was a picture inside the abdomen that was required and there was a fair sized incision made and held open by retractors. I aligned my camera from over the top and went to focus it. Everything was steamed up! I was very anxious. If I took the shot that had been carefully prepared for, would I get the pictures I intended or not? I was tempted just to press the button and go away. Anyway they would not know till it was developed. However I had long since learned that you only get one chance in most clinical photography and the hard fact was that the picture I had got was of a misted screen, no details of the operation. I decided to check everything again. I realised that looking through a lens in a warm, dry operating theatre was different to being set up for focussing vertically over the abdominal cut and only about six inches above it. It was steam from his belly that was causing the trouble. I turned to the surgeon and told him the position. He wanted his photographs. He turned round to the staff – "Open all doors" he said, and they did. There was the patient already opened up with a circulation of air going through the theatre! I hastily wiped and dried the lens and I could see when I re-positioned it that I had a lovely clear shot of his internal organs. I quickly took it and then the other shots I was detailed to take. "All is well, Sir." He had the doors shut and continued the operation. Ever since then I have been a little less confident about what happens when you are under a general anaesthetic!

The war progressed, if that is the correct word. The bombing was a little less, overall, but London was still being attacked regularly. One short weekend leave a shipmate who lived there said he would like me to go up and stay with his family. He lived in Croydon. I was pleased to do so. We arrived home on the Saturday morning and I was introduced to his family. "Mother" said he, "We're going to a dance tonight." "Oh no you are not," she said, "The sirens will go at 7:30pm and the raid will start about 8pm, and by then we shall all be in the air raid shelter." She proved to be accurate. It happened every evening at that time and everyone acted accordingly.

Come the Saturday evening and sure enough at about that time the sirens wailed. All six of us moved down into the shelter at the bottom of the garden. They were called Anderson shelters after the minister who devised them. They

Winton Cottage, King's Sombourne, June 1942.

were, in effect, a hemisphere of thick steel that was half buried and then well covered with earth. They were very effective against all except a direct hit and although we all felt vulnerable in an air raid, a direct hit was not very likely. The space inside was about twelve feet long and ten feet wide; a tight squeeze for six when you had often to stay there for hours, maybe all night. Everyone took flasks of tea with them, or whatever they preferred, and perhaps something to read as long as the light didn't show from the outside. When the night bombing began in earnest Londoners began to drift down into the underground railway stations - the tube. At first the authorities weren't very pleased about this and they tried to stop it. However the natural need for a safe place swamped them and after a while they stopped all the night trains and encouraged people to use them. Soon friendly groups were formed and they met every night at the same place. Some played music for singing and many friendships were formed. Sadly on a few occasions a bomb fell near enough to blow up both tube and people. In fact it was truly amazing that for about four years the general populace could work, shelter, do ARP, or fireman's duties on many nights and then go to work again in the morning. To do this they might have to walk there, in some places over mounds of still-burning masonry. The air raid wardens, fire services and other similar workers, many of them volunteers, were wonderful and kept the country going. The general preparation that was made pre-war was excellent. There were inevitably various things which happened which hadn't been foreseen. As an example, you couldn't fight fire with a hosepipe connected to a broken water main! These problems had to be overcome.

To continue the details of my weekend visit, my mate took me round some of the local interest points during the daytime and on Sunday evening I had to return to the hospital. I was on a short weekend; get back before midnight. He was on a long weekend; back by 1100 Monday morning. He saw me to Waterloo station, where I boarded a waiting train. This was about 2000 on Dec 29th and the air raid was just beginning. We were due to move off at 2015 for Portsmouth. This we did but we only went about two hundred yards, waited there for about half an hour and then moved a few more yards. This went on and on. Eventually we reached Battersea Power Station and waited again. All this time the high explosive and firebombs were dropping around us. It was the night during which a photograph was taken of St. Paul's cathedral surrounded by smoke and flames. This was in all the papers and has since become a favourite picture of wartime London. I once again just hoped I would be lucky, and I was. Eventually we moved far enough to leave the city and gradually rolled away into the countryside, reaching Portsmouth about three hours late. I still believe that luck is the most important part of life.

Time was rolling by and eventually I was told that I would have to be ready for draft in three weeks time. Enid was also in the same position but we were able to spend some time together at her home and at mine. The next weekend I went down to her home, a lovely thatched-roof cottage in the Hampshire village of King's Somborne, about twelve miles south of Winchester, just alongside the wonderful River Test valley. We talked things over and decided it would not be right to be married, although many couples were doing that in similar circumstances. We did, however want to have some sort of link because I was going to sea and didn't know for how long I'd be away, or even if I would come back at all -or perhaps even worse, come back injured. We decided to get engaged. I had to get back to Haslar by midnight and we agreed that we would meet each other in Winchester on the Monday afternoon, when I had shore leave, to buy a ring. That morning I checked the train time to Winchester and found that my shore leave began just an hour too late to catch it. After much thought I went down to see the Chief P.O. in charge of the regulating office. I thought I'd stand a chance of getting out an hour earlier because I was Captain of Haslar Hospital's very successful football team and he ran it. I knocked on the door and went in and said, "Chief, I've got a problem!" "What is it lad?" "I became engaged to be married last weekend." "Bloody hell lad, you have got a problem, haven't you!" He gave me permission to get out in time to catch the train.

There is one more particular memory I have of that time. When I went over to see Enid's parents she came to meet me and guide me to the right place. We parked the car in their front drive and walked towards the house. I was amazed to see coming towards me my hopefully future father-in-law in full army Officer's uniform. I didn't know whether to say "Hi, Dad" or salute. I played safe, saluted him and said, "Good Morning, Sir." He was a Captain and had re-joined after service in the First World War.

My next trip was to my home with Enid so that my folks could at least see the girl who was to be my future wife before I went away and so that, hopefully, she might visit them occasionally whilst I was away. After a leave of a few days I went back to Haslar and the time came for me to move on to my first ship. This was accomplished by a draft to HMS Victory, that is Portsmouth barracks, and then by rail to Liverpool and on to the docks. There I saw a large good-looking ship painted all in white except for two or three large red crosses on its sides and funnel. I learned afterwards that she was a ship newly built for the Java-Japan trip. She was completed just about the time when the Japanese attacked Pearl Harbour and although she was barely ready for sea the ship's Captain decided that rather than be captured he would cut and run for the USA. This he did using a school atlas to navigate right across the Pacific Ocean – a remarkable bit of seamanship. In the USA it was finished off as a hospital ship and sent across to Britain. We were its first medical crew for its first hospital trip.

Chapter 6-

JOINING THE TJITJALENGKA
TO GO TO HALIFAX

We stayed in Liverpool for a couple of weeks finishing off and getting inboard the last stores. This mostly meant fetching large heavy packages up the gangway! There was a notice on the board asking for anyone with an interest in cinema work. I checked up and found that we had a full sized cinema on board to entertain ship's crew and patients and they needed two sick berth staff to train to use it. I volunteered and with one of the Petty Officers I went several evenings a week to be taught at a Liverpool cinema. It was very interesting. There were two projectors in sync. in the projection room at the back of the auditorium. One was used whilst the other was off. When you came near the end of a reel one man took the one being used and the other man stood by with the spare projector, on which the next reel had been clipped. When you were nearly at the reel's end you looked for a spot which appeared at one of the top corners of the screen. When this became visible the other projector was switched on. When the second spot appeared the light was switched on the second projector at the same time as the light and power were switched off the first one. If done well there was no noticeable break in the picture. In culmination, we two sailors actually gave an evening show at the cinema on our own.

Eventually we moved out into midstream. My first idea of what it was really like to be on a ship. You could only go ashore in a boat. This was when we learned what a disadvantage it was to be without one. After a couple of days we moved back alongside to pick up some casualties that we were repatriating to Halifax, Nova Scotia. I was put in charge of a large eighty cot ward that was below the waterline. This meant that all washing and lavatory facilities were on the deck above. We also learned that many of the casualties were in fact not really injured. It had been decided that a number of soldiers who were disruptive were to be sent back to Canada in the hospital ship. This was against the rules and we could have been sunk by the Germans had they been aware of this. It also meant that we had to put life jackets on them and carry them on stretchers onto

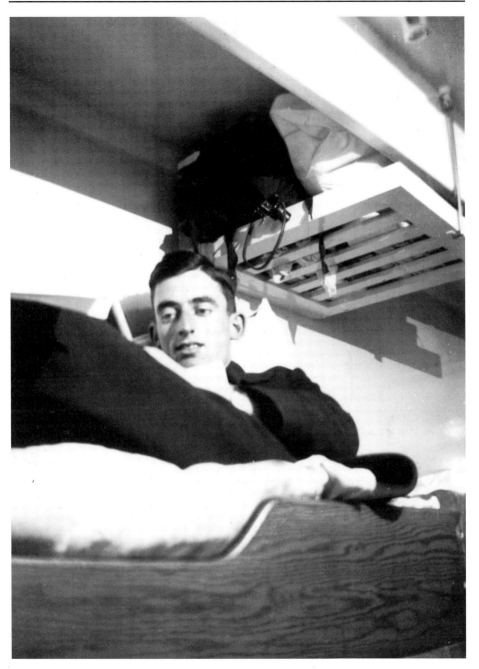

Jack Woolman in cabin 5 on HMHS Tjitjalengka on the way to Halifax, 1942.

the ship. They were a bit rough and didn't believe in discipline. If a sergeant said to one of them, "Go and do so and so" the man was just as likely to refuse as to obey. The man would say, "No I won't." The sergeant would reply, "Come on then, up on deck." They would go up and have a fight. If the sergeant won the man would go and do the job. If the man won he wouldn't! We learned afterwards that our Captain had been told that if he managed to get them home without a mutiny everyone would be satisfied. They were also playing a gambling game all over the ship in spite of the fact that it was forbidden. There was one time when I was told that the Captain was coming shortly, to do an inspection. Now a Captain's inspection is a major event in the Navy. Everything has to be clean, tidy and shipshape and above all silent with everyone at attention. When he appeared at the top of the gangway leading down to my ward I yelled "Attention in the ward!" Expecting everyone to obey. No one took a bit of notice. Whilst our staff stood at attention the soldiers went on just as they had been. One man was cutting hair in the middle of the ward, some were asleep, others chatting. After a few minutes the Captain looked very uncomfortable and called "Carry on please." Had it been a normal navy routine all would have obeyed instantly.

Eventually all were inboard and we sailed that evening; my first sea trip in the Navy. After we had sailed we were told where we were going but firstly we were calling at Belfast. We went on steadily through darkness. It was very

Hospital football team (Jack is extreme right 2nd row).

peculiar to be the only ship lit up. We were completely at the mercy of the Germans who could have sunk us whenever they pleased. The routine was that hospital ships were distinctively marked and lit when they sailed. The Germans were told their course and destination and were supposed to leave them alone.

Next morning we were anchored in Belfast Lock and then at about 1100 we sailed out into the Atlantic. Unfortunately we ran into a bad storm and very rough seas. The ship was bucking and kicking in spite of its 11,000 tonnes. One minute we were on top of a wave, perhaps thirty feet high and in the distance was a convoy of ships, the next either you or they were in a trough and you were completely alone. That afternoon I was on duty. My ward had in it about eighty beds filled with men, all laying on their beds and all sea sick into buckets alongside them. Many of the sick berth staff were also afflicted because they hadn't been to sea for some time and weren't used to it. I felt dreadful but I wasn't going to be sick and let the soldiers see me. I hung on and managed but when it came near to 2100 and time for my relief to come I was mighty glad. Then about 2030 a messenger came round from the regulating office. "Woolman you have to do a middle watch (2400 to 0400) on such and such a ward. The night duty man has gone down with sea sickness." That was the last straw and the beginning of my learning of what it was like in the Navy. Don't try to be heroic, keep your head down. Gradually the gale eased and we sailed comfortably on. My accommodation was very good. Two of us shared a small cabin with one bunk over the other and we each had a locker and a couple of drawers. Quite civilised.

When the soldiers recovered they began to move about the ship and found the canteen. There they were able to buy bottles of lemonade. When they had drunk them they dumped the empty bottles under the bed and left them. When we cleared up after the trip we collected sufficient bottles, which we returned to the canteen at tuppence each, to buy enough cigarettes to keep the staff going for a week, and I was at that time smoking about sixty per day. We could buy them at twenty for sixpence.

After that bad start all went quietly on across the Atlantic. Sometimes I used to stand on deck at night, see the dark water swirling by us and wonder how long I'd last if I was dumped in that! Our route to Halifax took us a little further north than Britain and when we reached the coast of Nova Scotia we turned south down to Halifax. This meant that we passed over the Newfoundland Banks, which were shallows famous for their cod fishing. As we sailed through we saw many boats so engaged. The system used was remarkable. There was a mother ship to which many small, almost canoe-like, boats were attached. In each was a man standing up holding a line in each hand. On every line were about seven large hooks, unbaited. He was letting the lines alternately sink down and then sharply pulling them up. This speared fish, often about three or four per line. There were so many fish in that area that you couldn't miss them. It is a cold reality that I understand there are now no fish left and the industry has closed down.

We proceeded to Halifax. To enter you have to sail up the estuary and I shall always remember it. It was a lovely sunny October day, the water was blue with speckles of white and the shoreline background consisted of conifers fronted by yellow gorse; truly beautiful. There were other surprises to come. First, however, we had to disembark our passengers. The genuinely injured were transported to hospital. The fit ones who were on board illegally were again put onto stretchers and carried off by our staff, the effort not being popular! After that we had to collect all the bottles and clean up the ward. One fact, which soon became noticeable, was that there was no heating in the ship. It was built to operate in tropical waters and not Newfoundland in October. It was noticeably below tropical temperatures and we could tell! However it was excellent in the daytime.

We were operating by the usual four-watch system; that is red and green with each broken further into Port and Starboard. My turn to go ashore came round and off I went with one or two of my regular mates. What a shock we had when it was dark. After having endured three years of blackout, when it was an offence to show even a glimmer of light, we were confronted by what seemed to be a wonderland. No blackout at all, and shops and restaurants just full of everything. We were in Halifax for about two weeks and never really became accustomed to it.

My main purchases were presents for the family and Enid. I also remember the food that was available. After the routine baked beans, egg and sausages that we had become used to from the canteens in Britain, it seemed impossible. On my first trip ashore we had a marvellous meal and for pudding I ordered apple pie. The waitress said, "Apple pie and ice cream? " I replied, "No thank you. Just apple pie." It so amazed her that anyone could eat apple pie without ice cream she could hardly bear to serve it. To me, I'd had a big meal and the apple pie was just about all I could manage. In England that's just about all we had, either apple pie or ice cream. There wasn't much ice cream about either.

There was another interest that I was able to continue with, photography. Just as with food and goods there was a normal peacetime stock of photographic material. I suggested to one of the Petty Officers who worked in the X-ray department that we stocked up with film, paper, chemicals and the like and started what on ship was known as a photo firm. He agreed to help and use his darkroom facilities and we were soon well kitted up. Being the Navy however you couldn't just do things like that however useful they may have been. You had to submit to the office an application which said "Requisition for permission to begin a photo firm", together with your personal details and what the prices were to the ship's company. In due course this was returned either marked not approved and that was the end of it, or approved subject to details. We had then to submit those, prices, print sizes etc. We were ultimately approved. There was an additional warning. "No material from the ship's darkroom approved." Since we were already stocked up, this didn't matter although we always had to remain aware of it. It is a routine matter on navy ships for individuals to set up firms like that. Some cut hair, some mend shoes and it benefits everyone on board.

You would imagine that buying presents for Enid and the family was an ordinary routine matter, but it certainly wasn't. Firstly what would they like? There was everything anyone would want in the stores, just like peacetime. When you recalled what it was like at home, with everything limited by rationing, it was so very difficult to select from so much. In England even clothes were on coupons. I recall one evening ashore when I had decided to buy some underclothes. I didn't dare risk top clothes. I'd have been wrong on colour or size, I'm sure. Problem one, what size? I went, with obvious embarrassment, to a pleasant looking young lady and explained the problem. "What size would your young lady be?" I'd no idea so she pointed in turn to the many and varied girl assistants. "Like that one?" "Not so tall." "That one?" "Too big." And so it progressed. Eventually I settled on one which to my memory seemed about right and so I hopefully bought various items for Enid. The final hurdle to sort out was whether or not to risk sending them there and then over to UK and risk them being sunk by U-boat attack (which was very likely at that time) or carry them with me until I got home, not knowing how long that would be. Finally I decided I would carry them with me. I carried them for three and a half years! When I eventually returned, the presents had joined various other items, such as Indian carvings, which I bought as time went on. They all nestled at the bottom of my kitbag and were mostly in reasonable condition when I got back.

The next concern we had was what our fate was to be. We knew that we were destined to go tropical because a ship with no heating was certainly not intended for arctic waters. We also knew that if we were needed in the arctic they would send us there without compunction! Another pointer was that we had been issued with tropical gear before we left UK.

Eventually we sailed from Halifax, empty of sick cases. We were certainly not carrying any this trip. We were occupied with cleaning and adjusting or what we knew as "shaking down." After we had been at sea for a couple of days, and the weather as we went southeast became warmer, we found that we were going to Freetown, Sierra Leone. It also eventually leaked through that we had been destined to go to North Africa where the Allies, joined now by the Americans, were to make a landing. For some tactical reason it was decided that we wouldn't be needed and so we were diverted to Freetown. The landing in North Africa was a success and probably a turning point in North Africa.

It is surprising how quickly you forget you are on a ship in the middle of the ocean. One morning, however, I was a little perturbed when I saw a seaman climbing over the side and, apparently, dropping into the sea. I checked to find what had happened to him and was pleased, and thankful, to find him standing on the anchor, painting the ship's side.

At about this time the Surgeon Captain mustered all hands to give us a general outline of his attitude and what he expected of us. It soon became obvious that we were of no consequence to him. It was on the lines of "You are a new ships company. I expect you to run an efficient ship, obey orders and that means do as I say. If anyone steps out of line they will get the dirty end of the stick." He was in charge for two years out of what was to turn out to be a three and a half year draft. During that time the only person on the ship who mattered was him, and this applied to the Officers and Nursing Sisters too. I have never before or since seen such a heartless bully. If I could describe him more strongly I'd do so. He began at Liverpool although we didn't at that time realise the implications of it. Whilst we were finishing storing ship we were supposed to have two motor launches delivered to us. One was for the Captain and Officers and one for the sick berth crew. Unfortunately the Captain's hadn't arrived when we sailed. He therefore took ours and left us without one. At that time we didn't understand the implications. Even if we had we could not have done anything about it. The ship was to spend most of its time tied up about half a mile from shore in big estuaries acting as the hospital for our Eastern fleet. Thus we had no way of getting ashore or back when we were off-duty. This could have meant days and days of being ship-tied. No football, cricket, swimming or any change of scenery. We had to manage by begging a lift from any other ship's boat that happened to come alongside on its way ashore and when returning we had to do the same. We also received much help from the merchant Officers who ran the ship. The full effect of this situation became apparent later in the trip. In the places to which we were going in the tropics when we were off-duty we could, if able to get ashore, go for a swim, go to a wooden hut called the canteen or play sports. These were our only recreation. On board, below deck, the temperatures often didn't go below 84°F day or night, and were often much higher. The record was 120°F under our awning on top deck.

After about eighteen months we discovered that we had been supplied with a table tennis table before we sailed. There was plenty of room to put it up and so we cheerfully put in a chit, "Requisition for permission to erect the table in such and such a place." After about two weeks a reply came back, "Not approved." There was nothing we could do. However after about three months we risked another request to use it. Again came the reply, "Not approved." This time, however, there was an additional item. "If this request is made again, disciplinary action will be taken." All the time the Captain was in charge we had no table tennis table. When he left we re-applied to the new Captain and in about a week it was granted and we were also granted use of the ship's boat when available. There were many other instances of his disgusting character. There was one occasion when one of the Nursing Sisters arrived at the shore end of a long jetty where we normally landed or took off to return. The Captain had just reached his boat, the only one available. He looked and saw the Sister then went

North West Arm, Halifax, Nov 1942.

into his boat. "Cast off!" he told the Bo' sun. The Sister was left on the jetty at about 1600 hours and had no way of returning to the ship except by begging a lift. This she eventually did after about two hours.

There was another instance when he was about to return to the ship and a black shore based rating in Freetown ran down to his launch with a message for him. The lad, in order to hand it to him, had to place one foot on the side of the launch. The Captain leaned across and hit his leg, quite hard, with his cane. "Get off my launch" was all he said. This kind of behaviour continued in many ways all through his turn of command. Everyone including the Officers hated him. The padre had been ordered not to visit our mess deck, a quite improper restriction that he obeyed.

There were two Officers who stood up to him and they were US Navy. He couldn't bully them at all.

In theory there is a freedom for everyone to make an official complaint, if they want to do so. The first difficulty is that obeying orders is given such a high priority that it would be amazing if a ratings complaint against a Captain was upheld. There is also the fact that some of the King's Rules and Admiralty Instructions known as KR & AI were drawn so broadly that it would be possible to find a charge against any one if authority wanted to and a rating would have little chance, especially in war time. In practice, if I had put in a complaint, I would probably have been drafted to a submarine in the Indian Ocean before anything else could get through.

After a few days, during which the weather became warmer and warmer, we were told that from tomorrow morning we would wear tropical rig. This meant that it would be shorts and shirts for everyone, any service or rank being indicated by a blue badge on a white background. These all had to be sewn on and that evening there was a great deal of scuffling and swearing as we hastened to be ready, otherwise we wouldn't have been 'properly dressed'. For that you could be 'in the rattle' and be punished. Somehow all was made ready.

The next morning we dressed and went to duties, it was an absolute riot. There were fat ratings with too-tight shorts, thin people with too loose shorts, tall ratings being nearly strangled, and short people who were almost hidden! These clothes were the ones that had been thrown at us from the clothing store when we were in HMS Victory, Portsmouth. Some people swapped with others where sizes suited. Some shortened shorts or shirts or lengthened them as the case required. In a remarkably short time, things settled down to normality. We even became used to each other's podgy or boney knees! We hung our discarded clothes in our lockers, not to use them again for three years.

This was the first time I had been in the tropics and I found it fascinating. We soon learned that sea gulls were really land gulls. They only followed us for a few miles out to sea and were not seen again until we got quite near to land again. This was compensated for by a number of (to us) fresh species - various terns were beautiful and frigate birds fascinating. One day I glanced out of the porthole and there was a large whale floating by just a few yards away. The sun shone and the sea was blue and all was well with our world, almost; there was still a war on. Another cheerful thing was the food and messing facilities. When we first joined the ship it was excellent. No poor bread like in England. Instead, Merchant Navy Stewards served beautiful smooth white slices. They were not up to the degree that Officer's Stewards operated at, though. They were ratings trained by the Navy for the job, but quite wonderful for us compared with warships or barracks. This little bit of heaven lasted as long as stores remained. More about that situation later.

On a hospital ship we were in a different situation to a warship. The hospital, staffed by all RN staff, was transported by the ship, which was manned by the Merchant Navy, stopping for a while at any necessary fleet base to be a hospital for it. The ship's officers were able to be more relaxed with us than RN officers. All doctors were officers. Some took advantage of this and some did not. I soon learned that doctors were people and, as with any other organisation, some were more capable than others.

Other interesting diversions were the talks we were given on living in the tropics, or almost surviving in the tropics. Being in most cases, 'hostility only' ratings we had little or no idea what the difference was. These talks were very good. They warned us about all the pests and diseases and the ways to minimise them. You couldn't avoid all of them, as we learned over a period of time. Gradually, at about twelve knots, we moved on and one day we were told that we were due to reach Freetown the next afternoon. This we duly did and I learned that it was no easy matter to pick up a pilot when entering and leaving port. Royal Navy ships may use a pilot but don't have to. Of course, if a ship's CO took it in without a pilot, and did something foolish like running it aground, he would have to take responsibility. We dropped anchor some half mile from shore. We could see a busy port that looked after a part of the Atlantic fleet with warships coming and going frequently. There was, in fact, a small single storey RN hospital ashore but it was not anywhere large enough for wartime needs. We were destined to be tied up, taking the position of main hospital for about six months whilst the RNHS Oxfordshire, which we were replacing, went home for a refit.

Chapter 7-

FREETOWN

I shall always remember my first shore leave at Freetown. I'd never seen an African country before and it was fascinating. There was a well-kept area of single storey houses where the better off people lived and a much poorer area of squalor, which was the original Freetown, called the village. This was a muddle of people, huts and open fronted stores. We were warned about it and were not supposed to go through it either to the shore or to the better area. We mostly did do so because it meant a much shorter journey. We learned, however, that we must keep our wallets and any valuables well protected. This was difficult because we were in tropical rig -white shirt with one top pocket and white shorts with two side pockets. I was rudely awakened when, after two or three times traversing the village, we became a bit careless. I had left a fountain pen in my top pocket and was walking through, chatting with my mates when I became aware of two lads, probably about ten years old, running hard towards me from some distance ahead. I didn't take much notice as they ran past me and vanished into the crowd. It was only afterwards I realised my pen had also vanished into the crowd. You have to learn the hard way!

Through the village ran a rather polluted stream. At one point, where there was a small waterfall, the local women used to do their washing. Due to the fact that they were "topless" and their method of cleaning meant swinging a piece of clothing over their head and bringing it down hard onto the rocks, this soon became known as "Swinging-Tit Falls."

I was appointed, with others, to be a gangway watch keeper. This meant that there were always two ratings there. One was in charge and the other rating acted as a runner to take any callers to whichever part of the ship they required. We also had another job, calling out any boats coming towards us as soon as they were within hailing range. You took a deep breath, concentrated and yelled, "Boat ahoy!" The coxswain of the boat would then reply "Passing" or "No, No" which meant that he was coming alongside but had no flag Officers aboard, that is the big noises, or "Yes, Yes" he was coming alongside and had a flag Officer aboard. This sent a flutter through the watch keepers who had to be sure they saluted properly and took them to their destination as speedily and as efficiently as possible. If not, you were likely to hear further about it from your own Captain. During the night we were supposed to be awake and alert. We did, however, have a chair each and used to sit on this and sometimes take turns to have a nap. I remember one occasion when the Duty Officer suddenly appeared and I was smoking a cigarette, which was quite forbidden. In a panic I threw it over the side. To my horror if floated gently and slowly down towards the water emitting so many sparks you'd have thought it was a firework. He simply said, "All correct, Woolman?" "Yes, sir." I thankfully replied and he went on his way, bless him. There is a heart to the system but it must be unofficial. Had there been a senior Officer with him he would not have hesitated to report me, or he himself would have been reported. The senior Officer would also have had to report the junior or he may have been in trouble if he hadn't acted correctly, or as we used to call it 'pusser' (for Pursar). For example when you were in any doubt you acted pusser, that is according to KR & AI (King's Rules and Admiralty Instructions). If you could do that and prove it you were fairly safe from being reported.

There were a few recreations for off-duty time. Football, cricket and swimming if we could get ashore. If you didn't want them you could go to the wooden hut called "The Canteen" and drink. You always had to be careful if you

Mufulomoo, Sierra Leone. This is "The Village" and the little creek (right of centre) is where "Swinging-Tit Falls" were.

had overdone the drink as once you went back to the ship you must not be noticeably drunk. This meant that you had to recover your balance sufficiently to walk up the gangway, stand to attention and salute the quarterdeck and remain upright until you vanished down between decks. You'd be surprised how adept you became at the manoeuvre. However drunk you were ashore, provided you didn't make it obvious or fall about, you would be helped along by your mates, one under each arm if needed and made to appear sober. Although this was the official attitude, there were in fact other hazards, even when safely aboard. One morning when we went on deck there was a rating asleep in the scuppers (in effect a shipside drain to take away water from the deck). We went over to tell him that it was time he wasn't there and found that he had become fixed to the scuppers by his hair. When he had dropped off to sleep his hair had become stuck to the tar, which was still warm from the previous afternoon. He couldn't move at all. We had to release him by cutting his hair a bit at a time and eventually rolling him out. This was accompanied by the usual ribaldries about his family background.

The same 'golden rule' applied to the Naval Police who used to patrol the shore area, wherever you were. It was simply to keep everyone out of trouble, if possible, but not to the extent of getting your self into trouble. In passing, I will mention that the US navy patrols were very efficient in breaking up rough stuff. They had short and very effective truncheons with which they used to hit anyone who was causing trouble on the head. They went down quite quickly and were bundled into the accompanying van.

Our shore leave was afternoons only, so that we had much less chance of catching malaria. One day we did normal shifts on duty, the next day we were off from 1300 till 1700. There was not much danger from mosquitoes during daylight hours. I soon worked out that if we lengthened our afternoon shift to six hours it gave us an extra afternoon off. Because a six hour shift instead of a four hour one was quite heavy in tropical heat it was harder to persuade my fellow watch-keepers of its great benefits, other than the Warrant Officer who was responsible. He didn't really care so long as there were always two on duty and we didn't bother him. We did agree, eventually. Those who wanted to play football or cricket were naturally in favour anyway.

Before we sailed from Liverpool I decided to take my football boots with me, just in case I had a chance to play anywhere, so when I was told there was going to be a game against a local team I was pleased. The only problem was that the temperature was around 90°F and I didn't know if I'd be able to stand it.

I went, of course. Imagine my surprise when we dropped out of our lorry to

48

find the pitch was not green grass but hard sun-baked mud and the touchlines were made of concrete protruding about an inch above ground. To add further indignity there were no nets on the goals. This mattered because I hit a long shot from about twenty yards, which went beautifully into the top corner of the goal. The referee who was well down the field and who was my best mate said it had gone over the top and gave a goal kick. After the game I explained to him how wrong he was! There was also the time when I was hit in the face by the ball. When I got back on my feet I happened to glance along the touchline and to my amazement it was swinging to one side just like a snake. The heat obviously wasn't doing me any good and I vowed never again to play football in the tropics. It goes without saying that I did. The next game I played in was not so bad, and eventually I got used to it. On one occasion where we had a match, the lab took a urine test before and after the game. We were told that it was a perfect case of nephritis with all sorts of cells and rubbish in the after-game test. It didn't stop us though.

Cricket, a game that I hadn't played much since school, because I preferred playing tennis, was also a great relaxation. I enjoyed playing but still had to have a go at my mate, Len Harris, because he gave me out "caught behind" off a ball that missed my bat and touched my shorts.

Left to right, Jack Woolman, Len Harris & George Wilson,
Freetown, Sierra Leone 1942.

49

Banana girl at Lumley Beach, Freetown, Sierra Leone, Jan 1943.

Swimming was very popular and there were some lovely beaches there. The biggest and most popular one was Lumley Beach. The naval authorities provided us with a lorry and took us the two or three miles to the shore. It was a long sandy stretch with beautiful waves and blue-water views. Coconut palms were abundant and at the far end was a village on the side of a small stream. Occasionally we used to walk down there and mess about in the fresh water. At that time I didn't have enough experience to separate fresh from clean water. I now realise what danger from infection we were probably in. Still, all's well that ends well. There were a couple of discoveries that interested me. One was when you dived under the water it was noticeably running in two different layers. The seawater layer had few fish in it whereas the other, of fresh river water, was full of the various tropical fish we see in tanks at home. Another item of appeal to us as first-timers was the girls who used to wander about the beach with a quantity of coconuts for sale. Naked to the waist we naturally found them interesting! There was one occasion when we saw one whom we had become on chatting terms with. She strolled along with a tiny baby slung over her back. We began to pull her leg about it. "Is it yours?" "Yes." "Bet it isn't." "Yes it is." "Look" she said, and squeezed a jet of milk out towards us to prove it. "Naval Officer came here," she said. She may have been telling the truth.

When we first arrived it was very hot, around 90°F or more. The hottest I experienced was 120°F under our awning and very humid. This caused us many troubles. Sweat rash caused by infected sweat glands looked like a million small red spots, mainly on our backs. The main discomfort was when you leaned back against a chair back, or similar. It felt as if a hundred needles were piercing your skin, and just to add to it another hundred when you sat forward again. Dhobi itch, dhobi being the term for laundry work, was also an enemy. It affected your groin particularly, but also any part where sweat collected rather than evaporated away. You lost the skin and suffered a red raw patch that really could be very painful. Just to complete the sweat problem was toe rot, when large areas of skin peeled off from between your toes due to damp conditions encouraging fungal growth. These problems were in addition to the usual infectious diseases to which you can be subject and virtually everyone suffered. So far as clothes care and laundry was concerned we were lucky. We just had to send them to the ships laundry where they were washed and sent back in excellent condition. We were also lucky in having a plentiful supply of water for washing and showering. This was because the ship was originally planned for the Java to Japan run. Water was expensive from one end and cheap from the other so they installed tanks which were twice as big as normal to do a double run. This made it particularly suitable for a hospital ship. In comparison, the warships had to ration water to a few hours a day.

After seeing the backdrop of the mountains behind Freetown for a while, a few of us decided we would like to climb it. At about two thousand feet it seemed right for the time we had to spare we could go ashore about 1330 and return about 1700; so off we set. It was cloudless at that time of the year, and very hot. The afternoon was definitely not the best time for mountain climbing, especially in normal RN kit, including cap. We found that there were fairly straightforward paths and it didn't present any difficult problems. We very much enjoyed the climb and the view from the top. We couldn't, however, do any further exploring because of the time available so we set off back. We didn't realise how much bush-type vegetation there was and we couldn't see very far ahead, nor around us at all because it was higher than we were. On top of all this we kept going into patches of elephant grass. It was a grass and elephant was very appropriate as it grew some seven feet high, rather like a bamboo. The main deterrent however was the fact that the leaf edges were like sharpened knives and you only needed to touch one as you went by to get quite a nasty cut.

We made our way down, successfully, until we came to a path division and didn't know whether to go to the right or to the left. There was a good stout branch above our heads at about six and half feet and I said I would pull myself up and find out which would be best. I was just about to do this when I saw a few frighteningly large ants. I checked the branch I was intending to catch hold of more carefully and to my horror I found it was covered along the top side with hundreds of them marching along from where I knew not, nor to where. I quickly gave up the idea of pulling myself up. We decided to go left and hope; at least we knew the way we were going was down and all eventually ended well.

I quite enjoyed my gangway duties although it meant frequent night duty. We did the usual watches on a twenty four hour basis, but I could get ashore three afternoons out of four, which suited me for cricket and football. It turned out that we had a much better team than could be expected from a ships company as small as ours, because we had a bowler and a batsman who normally played in the Lancashire league. We could always rely on one to bowl them out and the other to score the necessary runs! When I was off-duty but not going ashore I used to stand in for duty for the batsman, so that he could play a few extra games. It provided a change too, because he was a mental nurse and it meant I was looking after his ward and learning a bit about mental nursing. One thing I learnt was that I would not become a mental nurse! It was too demanding.

Of course, I'd had no training in this area, so I didn't know about the interesting aspects of it.

Slowly the time passed and Xmas was upon us. Still no mail arrived. We used to watch out for the Sunderland and Catalina flying boats that came in at intervals, because we were told that they brought in the mail. I never found out whether or not that was true. There was a clever innovation in connection with the mail. This was Aerogrammes (V-mail), simple nowadays but quite an advance then. You applied for a special letter form, which was about foolscap size. You wrote your letter or drew whatever picture you were able. It was collected as ordinary mail but then photographed on to film, which was taken home by air. At the other end a facsimile was made on to a letter of the original size. This gave a big saving in weight and bulk and speeded up the delivery.

It was decided to have an Xmas party, which is quite usual on ships or shore bases of the Navy. They asked for volunteers to organise it and I offered, as I was always keen on amateur dramatics. We had to write the acts as well as perform them but in wartime there were many very able performers in a ships company, so that you had experts in almost anything. For example we wrote a skit where Macbeth had to be admitted to a hospital ship, using as much Shakespeare as possible. We had one about a man who was somewhat ill in bed and surrounded by several pals and family. One side wanted him to go to the football match and the other to his friend's wedding. There was much vigour in the method of persuasion used. We had a ballet and a choir singing songs suitable for homesick sailors and, of necessity, both male and female parts were played by men, and very realistically too!

The Xmas party provided a heaven-sent opportunity to drink, already one of the favourite pastimes of many, if not most, sailors. It also allowed us to get in a few sarcastic points about the Officers and all that they engendered. Providing, that is, the things said were not personal or derogatory -not directly anyway! You couldn't say the Captain was a swine (or other suitable expression) but you could put a bit in about how a ship could be ruined by some awful unknown Captain! To fill in the gaps we had some very fine saxophone music from one of our American Officers. All in all, a good time was had by most of us. The few who didn't enjoy it couldn't quite remember what happened! There was one particular incident that anywhere else would have caused problems. One play required several fairies. That is, men dressed in tutus with gauze wings, all of which the ships company had to make (and very well too). When Xmas morning finally arrived and wakey wakey was piped at about 0630 we took stock of the situation. It was soon ascertained that two of the three fairies were not too happy.

An example of an Aerogramme sent to Jack's parents.

They had obtained some hooch spirit from somewhere, drunk too much and suffered accordingly. A few hours before the show was to begin one was deaf, the other one blind. This was not a very helpful thing for anyone who is scared of going on the stage anyway. Being on a hospital ship, with plenty of doctors, we were in quite a strong position to resuscitate them. Just what methods were used it is better to forget. After all, there was a war on. There was just one more problem. Half an hour before starting time one of the players was missing. Someone helpfully told us that they had seen him a little while ago unconscious on the floor down below. We swallowed hard and thanked them. In due course we found that this was indeed the case. He was well under the influence. We picked him up, took him up on main deck where the concert was being held, and gave him treatment. By the time his cue was near we had him on his feet, held him there and waited. Came the cue and we pushed him out on the stage. He took three steps, gazed round rather dimly, and then fell flat on his face. His entrance was a great success and added considerably to the enjoyment!

Lest you think all our time was spent in drunken fun it would be well to tell you something of the medical side. Although on a ship we had a true hospital, this in fact was simply carried round within the ship. There were the usual facilities, the laboratory dealt with any necessary tests, the optical department,

Three fairies still on their feet at the Xmas party, 1942, Freetown, Sierra Leone.

physiotherapy, X-ray, operating theatre, dental department and others fulfilled their usual duties. The wards were divided up into type as usual, medical, surgical, infectious & mental, with specialised doctors in charge. There were seven doctors and seven Nursing Sisters plus a senior Medical Officer and a Matron. The wards were run on a day to day basis from the point of naval routine and general care by the sick berth staff, with a Medical Officer and a Sister overseeing the nursing and treatment. This sounds a little cumbersome but it worked very well. Each knew where their demarcation line was and so far as my experience went there were no problems. In any case the doctors and Sisters were Officers, and the sick berth staff were ratings, and ne'er the twain could fraternise. There was a mixture of 'hostilities only' and regular Navy in both.

Our main cases were what you would expect when a number of men are gathered together. On the medical side we had hernias and damage due to accident and fighting, usually due to over drinking at shore canteens. The general routine was that when someone on a ship needed attention they reported to a sick bay. This varied from a surgery and at least one Medical Officer with a Chief Petty Officer plus adequate staff on a large ship to a rating only on a small one. Any cases which were beyond the ships sick bay were transferred to the hospital ashore, or if not available to the hospital ship. This included any men injured on the Atlantic run which were based in Freetown and so altogether included a very wide set of needs. On the medical side the mosquito borne diseases were common and dangerous, the main danger being from malaria. To minimise the trouble all the ships companies based in Freetown had leave finishing at about 1700 hours just before sunset, when the mosquitoes became active. Those based ashore had to wear long sleeves and long trousers during the evening. We still used to get many cases though, both benign tertiary and the much more dangerous malignant tertiary.

Apart from medical duties, swimming was the most favoured activity when off-duty. This meant walking from the jetty to the beach. If we went the official way, skirting the village, it was about a mile further. Naturally we used to make a wary way through it. This, besides being a bit dangerous, enabled us to enjoy the sight and experiences of a genuine native African village. There were many single storey huts either used as houses or selling stalls at the one extreme and at the other the very imposing brick-built Victorian style houses of the British civil servants and governor of the colony. There was also a large, fairly new, market hall where the imported food was handled.

Another entertainment if it appealed to you was prostitution. There were the usual, often attractive, girls and their men minders and then their advertising agents. These were small boys who came up to you as you were walking through calling, "Nice girl, school teacher you jig a jig my sister." Normally we used to just tell them to run away, in suitable words, but on one occasion when four of us were walking back to the jetty to return on board the ship, one of our group expressed a wish to see what the lad would lead to. Two of us said we didn't want to risk it but the other two did. Finally we went, on the understanding that the one lad would take advantage of the offer and we others would just go inside and wait for him. We followed the young lad some way to a row of quite reasonable wooden houses, only one of which was the brothel. Maybe some of the others were with different advertising agents! We were taken inside and introduced to an attractive black girl. By that time we had been in Freetown long enough to be able to separate out the good-looking African girls from the unattractive ones. Whilst she and the lad who was going to take advantage were chatting and we were just observing the situation a very large and powerful African walked through, obviously to let us know that the girl was well protected. Actually this was why we only decided to go along when the one lad said he'd go through with it. We knew what might have happened if we had led them on and then tried to walk out. Our mate went into another room with the girl and when he came out he paid his due and then we left. I must say that I thought he was very foolish. Being in the medical branch he should have known better what the risks were. I can honestly say that seeing patients with VD and the type of treatment they had then, kept me on the straight and narrow right through the war. There were enough difficulties to be faced without adding to them unnecessarily.

The shore base arranged a boxing competition one evening, inviting contestants from the ships companies there in the fleet. One of our mates took part so we naturally went ashore to support him. He did well but the part that really surprised me was that naval rules stated that there had to be dead silence whilst a round was being fought and then between rounds you could shout as much as you liked. What was really amazing was that several hundred men all obeyed it. There was dead silence. It made me realise just how strongly the feeling that orders had to be obeyed had been installed into us. The rule that had been so important was - if you don't agree with an order given by a superior then firstly obey it and afterwards complain officially. The result was that you just simply did as you were told. At the same time you learned to circumvent the most irksome instructions. The golden rule was not to be found out!

As time went by we became more and more anxious about our mail. In fact a few of us couldn't really take much more isolation from home. There was one man who suffered more than most because his wife was expecting a baby when he left England and he had heard nothing since October 1942. We were now into February 1943 and he could stand it no longer. One evening I was on gangway watch when he came along. He was a big, six-foot, fifteen stone man who up until the war had been a heavyweight boxer in the prison service. He was also one of the few men whom I came across who could get truly drunk but still stay on his feet. That evening he was in that condition. He came along to me and said, "Hello." I could see what state he was in. "What's the matter, Tubby, you look upset?" "Do you know what the Lieutenant Commander did to me this afternoon?" He said. "No Tubby. What did he do?" There was then a rambling few words about the supposed slight he had endured. He finished by saying, "I'm going up forward (Officers quarters on our ship) and I'm going to find him and I'm going to hit him with my left and I'm going to hit him with my right. He'll not treat me again like that." The important part of all this was that he had cracked under the strain of worrying about his wife and he meant it. The question was what could I do to stop him? He was much too big and strong to prevent him physically, so that wasn't on. I decided to talk him out of it, if I could. "Tubby, you can't do that you will be in trouble." "I can though and I'm going to, I don't care." I thought quickly and continued, "Tubby, they'll put you in jail if you do." "I don't care, let them do what they like." More quick thinking. "Tubby, if you go to jail they'll stop your pay." "Let them it doesn't matter." I was rapidly running out of things to say when I had a bright idea. "Tubby," I said, "Your wife's pay will be stopped too." There was a long pause for thought, and then he said, "What did you want to say that for. Now I can't do it." I breathed an inward sigh of relief and after a bit more chat to comfort him he went back to his mess. I've often thought of the time I saved Tubby from goodness knows what. In fact everyone was worried and upset until one day in March I came back from afternoon shore leave and couldn't believe my eyes. There were dozens of letters on my bunk waiting for me, dated from October to March! There was such a relief from tension on board it was almost tangible.

The question of worry was much more important than was realised in the early days of the war. I had another example, which happened late one afternoon when we received a patient from one of the ships who was completely unconscious. Nothing we tried would bring him round or give us any information. When the medical specialist was sent for, to our amazement, he lifted one leg and then loosed it. Instead of it dropping back onto the bed it stayed in mid-air. His next instruction was even more surprising. "Hit him hard on each cheek", he said. We did this and he became conscious and back to normal. It was a case of hysterical coma brought on by a long absence from home, during which he had become worried about his wife's behaviour and because he couldn't do anything about it his brain just went to sleep.

An occasion that caused much excitement and merriment was when we heard that there were one hundred ATS girls coming to live on board for a few days. At first we didn't believe it, but it was true. They were in transit from England to Cape Town and the ship that brought them to Freetown wasn't going that far and so they had to wait for a few days at Freetown before boarding another ship to Cape Town. It seems simple but remember there was nowhere ashore with sufficient accommodation for them. We had a spare ward and so they came. To understand the reaction this caused you have to remember that our lads hadn't seen an available white girl since we left Liverpool six months before. Naturally they were interested! The ward which was set aside for the girls was the one I had been in charge of on our trip over from Liverpool to Halifax Nova Scotia. The way down was by a wide wooden staircase that would have allowed a lorry to drive down it. This meant that if you stood in the ward at the top of the steps you could see almost the whole of the one below. News about this spread rapidly and that top ward had far more visitors from the rest of the ship than normal. The opportunity was just too good to be missed, especially as the temperature was around 80°F to 90°F and the girls off-duty wore little if any clothes. To complete the picture, they had to come up into a wash place and lavatories in the upper ward as there were no facilities down below because, if you remember, it was below the water line. They were with us for several days and the off-duty life on board was transformed. There were always a fair number of staff off-duty and many of them naturally took an interest in the visitors. If you wanted to you could find couples everywhere. In the lifeboats, under the lifeboats and at the back of anything which gave privacy. One night when I had to help my mate with the cinema he came into the projector hut when the film needed two of us to make a change of reel and then disappeared back to his girl friend. These few days were the highlight of the trip to that time.

One day the ship's Bo'sun came down to me when I was on gangway watch and said something like, "You tish me sing long way tickle Mary." A little confused I agreed, not really understanding the question. After I'd sorted it out I realised it was for him to sing the British ditty in a ship's concert, to celebrate their New Year in about a month's time. We learned that Chinese New Year was not on January 1st, like ours, but around the end of January or beginning of February. Lucky us, we had two sorts of celebrations! In both cases these were enlivened by a variety show, created and acted by the sick berth staff for our

New Year and the ship's crew for the Chinese New Year. In each case they were graced by the respective Officers and Captains in evening uniform.

The other noteworthy item of our Freetown stay was when yellow jaundice became troublesome. There were several ships companies affected and it was said that it was due to a faulty yellow fever inoculation given to us. Whether or not that was so, I don't know. They called it infective hepatitis. When I first showed symptoms they simply prescribed a fat free diet and light duty, which meant virtually every meal was a piece of chicken with some potato and carry on with my gangway job. Later they took more trouble, someone on one of the other ships affected had died and they were afraid there might be liability problems later on. The main effect so far as I was concerned was that as when had people go sick we hadn't anyone to replace them. This meant that we were working more and more duty turns until we were doing four hours on and four hours off all through the day and night. It was very trying, especially as I still had hepatitis and felt ill. Everything felt wrong from the top of your head to the end of your toes. However there was a war on and we made the best of it.

Chapter 8-

CAPETOWN

The next exciting thing was that there was a buzz that we were to leave shortly for Cape Town. This eventually proved to be true. All our patients were transferred to the hospital ship which was relieving us and away we went, empty of cases. It was a pleasant cruise for us. We were occupied by a certain amount of repair and maintenance jobs, lightened by deck sports and relaxation. The downside was that I still felt quite poorly, with aches and pains almost everywhere. I managed, as always, and we continued down the African coast to South Africa. By this time I was the colour of a canary and had to walk round Cape Town in this condition.

Whilst making this voyage, we passed by (but unfortunately were not able to land) on St Helena, where Napoleon was once imprisoned. Continuing on South we passed Tristan da Cunha, garrisoned in 1816 as a defence for St Helena. Obscure then, it was to be of world renown when its volcano erupted spectacularly in 1961.

The only worry we had was when we developed engine trouble and had to pull into Salhdana Bay, Namibia and anchored there for an unknown period whilst the ships engineers mended us. It may not sound much but when you are looking forward to a visit to Cape Town, the possibility of being laid up in what was just an inlet with a few wooden huts on shore wasn't very appealing. There was one aspect of life there that was of note, though. When we pulled the chain to flush the lavatory during darkness the pan was alive with pretty lights. On investigation we found that we used seawater for that purpose and the flush drew water from where we were anchored. This was so full of phosphorescent organisms that its glow lit the place up.

During our enforced stay I went down into the engine room to see how things were going, and found that our engine was quite like a giant car engine and was driven by several hefty pistons. The engineers eventually completed their task and we went to Cape Town. In fact we felt like real sailors now. Before, none of us, as hostility only men, had done enough sea time to really believe we were. No one ever said so but we were reminded from time to time by the sprinkling of regulars that "well, of course, the ink isn't dry on your signature yet. You don't really know what the Navy is." We reckoned by then that we had found out!

One morning we were due to arrive at Cape Town and were all very keen to be there. Out of the haze on the horizon was a dark bank of what may have been land or may have been cloud or as so often happens, both. Gradually it proved the first sight of South Africa. I shall never forget that first view of what to us was a new land. We came down the coast and turned round a point and into a bay that was like fairyland. In the foreground was blue water broken by white horses, in front of us was the magnificent Table Mountain with its table shape topped by the tablecloth of cloud and to the right the diminishing peaks of the mountains. At the foot of this magnificent view nestled Cape Town. It was about this time that I began to realise what a wonderful achievement our empire was and how much it had depended on the many naval bases all over the world, such as Gibraltar, Aden, Cape Town, Hong Kong and Sydney. They were all vital calling and maintenance points so very valuable, especially in the age of sailing ships, during which much of it had happened. You couldn't help but feel proud of it and its traditions.

Slowly we made our way to the harbour and tied up in the dockyard. No

On the top of Table Mountain, 1943.

62

liberty boat trouble here! We were only due to stay two or three days so we had to make the most of our shore leave. The routine on such occasions was that as much leave as possible was allowed. The Chiefs and Petty Officers reminded us that leave was a privilege not a right, the two watches taking it in turns. The first port of call for many of the lads was the nearest pub outside the dock gates. In fact many of them stayed there all day and saw little or nothing of the place they were visiting. My intent was to see as much as possible in the time we had.

I had heard and read much about Cape Town and the Table Mountain, so I took the first opportunity I had to go up to the top. The first afternoon a few of us walked round town and found our bearings. I well remember the silver leaf tree that is famous in that area and was growing in bushes about fifteen feet high. It had thick, hairy, moisture-retaining foliage, which reflected just as if made of silver. On our next shore leave I joined with another SBA, Len Harris, and we went up on the cable car. It was quite an experience since there are no intermediate supports, just one long cable fastened at top and bottom with a great sag in the middle. It was exhilarating to be on it going up to over four thousand feet. I had been looking forward to being on the top because it has some beautifully adapted and interesting plants. The top is as flat as it suggests from down below and is rocky but with slabs, each having some space round it and in the gaps grow these plants. It is very like our limestone pavements in Britain. The wind blow and harsh conditions prevent plant growth on the open tops but the plants grow down in the cracks. One striking phenomenon is the so-called Tablecloth. Seen from ground level it is a sheet of thick white cloud. At times the view shows Table Mountain with its flat square top and then suddenly thick, white cloud builds up and flows down about a quarter of the vertical side before it gradually dissipates. When it is in place you can well see why it is called the Tablecloth. If you are on top of the mountain it is rather a different experience. Suddenly, from nowhere, a thick fog forms. You can see little in front of you, certainly no view. A local hooter sounds a warning from the building on the top and everyone is supposed to stand still until it thins. You could, I suppose, walk into thin air!

After a couple of days we were ready to leave. We were delighted when they told us that we could collect any fruit we liked from dozens of cases piled on the dockside. It was the main fruit-producing time and none could be exported. It's an ill wind…! The weather was pleasant and there was no real problem with conditions. We had no patients on board and so it was almost a cruise ship! We followed the coast round the Cape of Good Hope and it seemed as if there was no life for hours and hours, miles and miles, just empty country. We were beginning to realise just what open spaces mean when outside Britain. We were told that our next port of call was to be Port Louis in Mauritius and eventually we arrived there. It seemed like a very agreeable and lovely island but we were only there for about four hours and so didn't get ashore.

On we went and round the east of the island where we sailed into an inlet, for what reason I have no idea. I do know that we were very anxious because when we attempted to come out again there was a strong north wind blowing and the inlet was so small that we couldn't get round and appeared to be in danger of being blown ashore. Only having one propeller we just couldn't make it and the ship's master had to make several forward and reverse runs. Eventually he managed it, but only barely, and we were very relieved when we slowly sailed out to sea again.

A comparatively short trip north took us to our destination, Mombasa, in Kenya. Although primitive by western standards it was a bustling and thriving port, and home to many of the dhows that travelled around the Indian Ocean.

We were destined to be there for about six months. I was also taken off gangway duties and put in charge of the main medical ward. I was glad I had passed my first badge whilst at Haslar because it gave me a very small move up the ladder as a leading sick berth attendant and qualified me to run the ward. I

The Tjitjalengka in Mombasa, 1943.

had at that time a staff of four sick berth attendants made up from three of us on port watch and two on starboard. That meant that we were able to go ashore on alternate days. Our working hours were 0800 to 1930 one day and 0800 to 1300 on the next day. It was, however, a couple of days before we had finished our preparations and were able to get ashore.

Mombasa was much more advanced than Freetown. The main streets were wide and on each side there were shops, generally of two storeys. The main trade was in woodcarvings, and there were some lovely examples using King Ebony, which was the heart wood of the tree and brown in colour with pale irregular rings. It was an old Portuguese town and trading post in the days before we took it. The most obvious structure was an old defensive fort named Fort Jesus. This was a small stone building, surrounded by a high wall, which covered a considerable area of ground. Naturally, as soon as we had the opportunity we walked up the hillock on which it was built to see what it was like. On the way up we passed some attractive flowers planted against the wall. At the time I didn't know what they were but later found they were named *Lantana camara.* I was also pleasantly surprised to find that at the top, inside the walls, was something in the nature of a park. There were tennis courts, which I was later able to play on. The fort was built so that an attack from the sea would

Fort Jesus, Mombasa, Kenya, 1943.

be very difficult. Another place of significance in the town, which we used to walk by, going to and from the ship was an Arab watchtower, which had been built in times past as part of the defences. It was cigar-shaped and about thirty feet to forty feet high. We used to call it Mombasa's phallic symbol.

Another artefact appealed to me. Although it was very simple it was true native art. It consisted of a set of two ashtrays about six inches across and two candleholders with a corkscrew column. The whole set was made from a lump of kissi stone (soapstone). The objects were carved out first and then they were burnt and polished, which left an attractive, glossy, black surface. It was a soft stone and patterns were carved out with ordinary tools that showed white stone beneath. These were amongst a number of items that I carried half way round the world in my kit bag!

On our first visit to Mombasa the malaria was usually benign tertiary. We subsequently returned there in our travels and in those few months there had been a marked change and the more dangerous malignant type had increased. This had been carried round from West Africa by the constant flow of troops heading around the Cape to the pacific area.

Another type of mosquito borne infection was dengue fever, rather similar to malaria but with a different pattern to the temperature sheet. Malaria had a

Nyali Beach, Mombasa, Kenya, 1943.

high every three or four days while dengue showed what we knew as a saddleback pattern. It went up to a high and fell again and remained thus till about four days later when it shot up again. The doctor responsible for my ward used to quiz us about many things as he did his rounds. One day when we were thus engaged alongside a dengue fever case he uncovered the patients abdomen to examine him and, turning to me suddenly, said, "What does that rash look like?" I didn't really know but I examined it carefully to give me time to think and said, "Scarlet fever, Sir." That was the right thing to say and my marks went up a bit. On another occasion we were looking at a case of amoebic dysentery and he said, "What is an amoeba?" By sheer good fortune I had just been reading a book on physiology and smartly answered, "A single cellular organism with a nucleus, Sir." My assessment record must have gone up a bit more! You had to appear capable of whatever was asked of you. Just do it or say it, don't appear indecisive. In fact he was a fine man and an excellent doctor. Surgeon Lieutenant R. E. King was his name. He was with us for most of the three and half years we were away and he taught me many things about tropical medicine in particular and medicine in general. This included such pearls of wisdom as "Of course they get ear infection. They use their towel to wipe their backside and then poke it in their ears." And "Don't ever put anything in your ear smaller than your elbow, Woolman." When he eventually left the ship to return home, a doctor whose only experience of tropical medicine was a few weeks course at the tropical disease centre in Britain replaced him.

Most of our cases were fairly routine, but there were always a few coming in who had problems. We sometimes just couldn't find out from our lab tests what was wrong. I still remember three ratings who were admitted about 1600 one afternoon. They all had very high temperatures and accompanying symptoms but we just couldn't find the cause of the trouble. We knew their livers were in danger but we couldn't find out why. We were all very worried and upset including Lieutenant King, who was called in to see them as medical specialist. The tension rose when one died about a couple of hours later, and another one a few hours after that. The death of the third seemed imminent. There was one particular blood test I would have asked for and for some reason Dr King had not. I went back to the ward in the evening, off-duty time but he didn't mind that. He was there and I said to him, probably several times. "Don't you think Sir that we should do a test for so and so?" It was only due to anxiety on all our parts but he, for the only time we were together on the ward, said sternly, "Petty Officer Woolman, I'm running this ward not you!" I'm sure he was right to pull rank on me but it was more surprising to me because he had let me do so much of the routine treatments and investigations myself. He used to trust me to take blood samples, give some injections and many other jobs because he was so busy at times. It all arose from the fact that we were required and trained to do many things beyond ordinary nursing. By then I had taken and passed my Petty Officer rate. This meant that on our release at the end of the war I should have the equivalent of an SRN grade but would have been trained to work above the grade. When we first joined we were told that we would have to learn to do anything in an emergency. On a small ship there may only be you. You would have no doctor or specialist help of any kind. You just had to do whatever was necessary yourself. That might include first aid, nursing, minor operations, radiography, dispensing and many other things. This wasn't as bad as it sounds. During my time in the Navy I was a chemist dispenser, a nurse, a radiographer, a clinical photographer, something of a laboratory technician, a cinematographer, almost a doctor, and as a Petty Officer I was also expected to maintain naval discipline and routine.

In Mombasa, we soon organised football and cricket with matches between the ships in port and occasionally with local shore teams. It was good fun, even though tropical heat was not conducive to English type soccer. It was whilst we were in Mombasa that we were given local leave. This was after about six months there. I made a trip to Nairobi, with a local family as host, for two weeks. I've always appreciated this. It isn't until you get away from the ship and mix with local families that you really begin to understand the habits and thinking of the country you are in.

One afternoon away we went. In a wartime Navy you never believe anything scheduled will actually happen until it does! We joined the steam train that went from Mombasa to Nairobi. In those days there was no air travel and only poor dirt roads as an alternative. As we left Mombasa we travelled very slowly through attractive hilly countryside. Our top speed when climbing (Nairobi is about six thousand feet above sea level) appeared to be about fifteen miles per hour. You felt as if you could get off the train at any time, pick some flowers and get back on again! Not only was it a steam train but it was also a very old wood burner, there was no coal to be had in those days and you really felt that it was stopping at times to cut some more wood. In fact it was a comfortable journey right through the night. There were adequate sleeping bunks folded away and we rather enjoyed ourselves. When they served our first meal, it was for tea. A neatly dressed African came into our compartment with notebook and pencil ready. What would we like? We had been warned that we must speak the native language as they wouldn't speak English. We had a dictionary, a bit of practice and much hope. We looked at the menu and hesitatingly said this and that in Swahili, finding that all its words end in a vowel. The lad wrote it all down in his little notebook. Just before he left I glanced at his notes and he had written it all down in excellent English without any difficulty. I found out in Nairobi later on that it was the rule that you should speak Swahili to all house servants; if they learnt to speak and understand English they would know too much about their employers. Swahili is one of the most widely used languages in East Africa.

Eventually at around 0700 the next morning we arrived at Nairobi station. When we first stepped onto the platform we were amazed at the lightness of the air. At that altitude the heaviness was so much less compared with Mombasa it was remarkable. We felt like running and jumping, almost reborn. A man named Shuttleworth who was hosting us met us at the station. He lived about five miles out of Nairobi along the N'gong road. You could see the N'gong hills away in the distance. His home was planned out in the style we think of as a holiday camp, with a quite large brick-built house as a centrepiece and then wooden hut dwellings all around. The main difference to a holiday camp was that the people who lived there were permanent residents who worked in Nairobi. After a few days we found that very few of the couples were married and this explained a

Nairobi, Kenya, 1943.

message we saw in Nairobi as we came through. It was written in large chalk letters and said, "Are you married or do you live in Kenya?" We soon learned the truth of that.

We were very well looked after and Shuttleworth was able to get an extra petrol allowance to take us around. One trip that we did was to a spectacular part of the rift valley. This is a geological fault that has created an almost continuous deep valley from Mozambique through East Africa to the Red Sea and the Mediterranean. It is a magnificent part of our heritage on earth. We went about thirty miles from Nairobi to a high plateau. The cliffs in front of us dropped many thousands of feet into the valley and at the bottom you could just make out where there was a vehicle moving from the dust cloud accompanying it. It was so deep that you could barely see the car. We viewed the area for a while and then drove back. When we reached home we found that we were covered in red dust. It meant we had to brush our clothes and have a shower. We were then given a beautifully iced drink whilst sitting on the house terrace. I was introduced to the commendable idea of a sundowner. After the heat and dust of the day what could be more pleasant?

We learned that Shuttleworth himself was a Yorkshire man by birth and had moved out to Nairobi about thirty years before. It was, as you would expect,

Nairobi, Kenya, 1943.

70

much more primitive then and he had some fascinating tales to tell. One remark he made was significant and told me much about the settler's attitude to the natives. We were discussing the social set up with apartheid in force and he said, quite seriously, "Of course, they are just like children and you have to control them. The trouble is you can't even flog them now!" It made me realise how things were and I couldn't help but feel that they gave them no dignity. For example one day whilst we were there, the police had caught two men, had arrested them and were taking them back to HQ. The sad part from my point of view was that they were marching them along the road for a distance of about three miles and had stripped them naked and put them in handcuffs. I definitely didn't like apartheid and although I felt that South Africa was the best part of the world I had seen I couldn't live there!

Another trip that we made was to an animal reserve that had been set up just outside Nairobi. It later became a National Park. This trip to Nairobi was the first time I had seen the larger wild animals, firstly from the train on the way up and then at this nature reserve. Naturally I was thrilled by it.

There was a good social life in the camp and we lads paired up with the regulars who took us out for extra trips and helped us to visit and understand Nairobi. There was a certain amount of bonding but not anything serious. Although one of our gang did apparently have an affair with the wife of Shuttleworth!

We used to go to dances in Nairobi, mostly at the Hotel Stanley. We experienced the licensing hours that meant that you were not able to buy a drink after 2300 but could stay until midnight to drink what you had bought. The result of this well-meant law, was that just before 2300 we bought as many drinks as we thought we would need and lined them up on the table. Inevitably we had bought more than we would have done, just to be on the safe side, and had to finish off several in the last quarter of an hour. I reckon that it caused more drunkenness than a no-restriction policy.

At last we had to face the return to ship. We had lived an almost civilian life for a couple of weeks and didn't look forward to discipline again. We had to leave near midday and were all gathered outside Mr Shuttleworth's house, except for one of us. "Where's Paddy?" said someone. "Oh," said Shuttleworth, "I expect he's gone to say a fond last farewell to my missus. It saves me a lot of trouble." Until then we didn't realise he knew!

We went back to the station and on to the train. This time, though, going several thousand feet down, not up, the train reached breath-taking speeds. It was probably forty or fifty miles an hour but with the same black wood smoke pouring out of the smoke stack. The journey was much the same except that a different time of day gave it a fresh appearance. What was very noticeable was that when we left the train at Mombasa the air was so hot and humid that we felt as though we were swimming rather than walking. However, being a while up in drier cooler air had eased our various skin and fungi problems considerably.

In Mombasa there is a fine stone-built cathedral and several of us went there to hear a choir singing. It was beautiful. Soon after that there was a buzz from the bunts (short slang for bunting tosser which was slang for a signalman and a relic of the days when flags were used for messages). It may seem an old fashioned way of communication but it was, in fact, carried out very quickly and efficiently when a fleet was in visual distance of each other and fairly secretive too.

Chapter 9-

DURBAN FOR A REFIT

We soon found out that we were to go to Durban for a refit, fumigation and bottom scrape. This meant a week or so in dry dock, no proper water supply or drainage and a constant barrage of noise day and night. There were so many machines in use most of which seemed to be used to bang against the sides of the ship that sleep was a luxury rarely attained. You would, for instance, intend to leave your cabin to try to escape the noise and find there was a paint sprayer just outside your door using a two-stroke engine. Apart from the noise you couldn't get out through the door for perhaps a couple of hours!

There were several excellent organisations in Durban that arranged outings for service men, ranging from a weekend to a week or more. The people were extremely kind and made us feel truly welcome. I remember one weekend particularly. We were told that we were, on such and such a date, due to fumigate the ship to clear out the bugs, cockroaches, ants and rats which all ships collect, especially in the tropics. Since they would use cyanide everyone had to leave. We would be given a long weekend leave. If we wished, arrangements could be made for us to be hosted in Durban or that area. Naturally I jumped at the chance, and fixed up to go to a lady and gentlemen who lived in Durban. There were, however, one or two snags, which arose when we began to organise ourselves. The fact that the ship was being fumigated meant that we couldn't leave any foodstuffs or tobacco in our lockers, or at least we couldn't eat any of it when we returned. We were able to manage most of our stores by using an empty tin that we scrounged and sealing it up with tape. That left quite a number of cigarettes. The problem was that when we were acting in our capacity as hospital ship out in the wilds, often for six months or more, the canteen which our supplies came from eventually ran out of some stores, including cigarettes. These were of prime importance for two reasons. During our hospital ship time we were anchored out in an estuary a mile or two off shore and getting ashore was difficult or impossible. This meant we had plenty of time to fill and smoking was the inevitable result. I was smoking about sixty cigarettes each day. At twenty for tuppence ha'penny to us this was affordable. To keep a safe supply in hand we stocked up with anything from two thousand to four thousand each to see us through any "drought" period. We couldn't waste this insurance policy. What were we to do? Several mates discussed it with me, each very anxious not to lose his lifesavers. Eventually I had the bright idea of taking them with us and declaring them at the gate. With some trepidation this was agreed. Four of us went down to the dock gates the next morning to go ashore for the weekend. There was the usual dockyard policeman checking as we went out. "Anything to declare?" he said. "Fifteen hundred cigarettes," I replied. He looked amazed. "You can't take that many" I explained to him what the difficulty was and why I couldn't afford to lose them. He thought for a bit, scratched his head and said "'Ere, stand aside." I did so. "Next," he said using his best authoritative voice. "I've got two thousand." "Stand aside." Number three came forward. "I've four thousand," said he. "Next," said the increasingly worried policeman. "Three thousand" said he. "Good God, what am I going to do with you lot!" Said the now floored policeman. "You know you can only take two hundred ashore for the weekend." I suggested we leave them with him and collect them again when we came back on board. At the thought of this he became even more panic stricken. He thought for a few minutes, looked right, looked left, looked all round, turned to us and said in a voice full of anxiety "'Ere, bugger off quick." Thus we saved our cigarette supply, an example of how you can

Durban, Natal, 1943.

floor the service personnel if you present something a bit out of the ordinary and not covered by Kings Rules and Admiralty Instructions. They just don't know how to deal with it. We cheerfully went ashore and had a very pleasant weekend.

Whilst in Durban I also had a very enjoyable week with a family in Johannesburg, named Metter. They hosted me and one of my mates and looked after us marvellously. Mr Metter was in the diamond mine business and he offered us the chance to go round a mine. I shall always regret that I didn't take the opportunity. It must seem very peculiar to anyone now but the difference between a private house with all its comfort and peacefulness and a ship life was so great and so soothing that all I wanted to do was to relax and read a book. The Metters were rather perplexed because we enjoyed short drinks, whereas the two men they had hosted the previous week had drunk them out of beer. They had stocked up heavily for our week and we hardly drank any beer! We had a marvellous week and a complete break from the Navy in the company of some lovely people. When the week was up we returned to Tjitjalengka and whatever the future held for us. I was particularly pleased when one day, some months after the war, the Metters unexpectedly looked me up at Cardah, my home. I tried to reciprocate but I couldn't match a week's heaven, which at the time it was, with a couple of hours unexpected visit.

The fruit stall, Bombay, India, 1943.

It transpired that we were to sail to Bombay to collect a load of African soldiers who had developed tuberculosis. They were walking cases, so there was no stretcher work. Because they were all TB cases they were not supposed to do any work. Normally, recovering patients who were fit enough did light jobs in the wards and enjoyed being occupied. This was easily adjusted to except for us cleaning the heads (bathroom and lavatories). This was proving difficult because a few of them had no idea how to use them and left them in a very poor state. Eventually we received permission to let them help us. This improved the situation as their peers soon taught miscreants better!

We were all looking forward to India. When we arrived we first saw the fine Gateway to India arch surrounded by other large buildings. Our first job was to clean and tidy up the wards and then we were allowed shore leave on the usual watch system. On this occasion, as sometimes happens, three quarters of the ships company were allowed ashore each day to give us a better chance to explore. I found that whenever a break in routine was possible it was allowed, probably because by then we had been away from home for about two years. My first visit ashore was always a new experience. I soon found that Bombay was quite different to Africa. It was very crowded, hot and untidy. At the same time it was a fine city and the buildings were imposing. Unfortunately there was a proportion of the inhabitants who, as they walked along, chewed betel nut and whilst doing so made a lot of red coloured saliva. This they rid themselves of by squirting it out of their mouths, usually achieving a considerable jet of red fluid. There were two problems with this habit. Firstly if you were walking along you had to keep a careful watch in case anyone hit you as they walked by and the second was that the walls of the buildings and the pavements were permanently stained dark red up to a height of about five feet. We were only in Bombay for a short time before our patients came aboard and we sailed off again for Mombasa. After a short stay in Mombasa we moved on again. We crossed the Indian Ocean and down the coast to Ceylon (now Sri Lanka). This was a long trip, much of it out of sight of land. We were occupied with cleaning and, where necessary, repairing our cabins and wherever we were needed.

I mentioned earlier the bugs which we collected. They were a real irritant. They sheltered and bred behind the bunk frameworks and when you went to bed if you didn't get to sleep quickly you felt them crawling over your head and face. Sometimes when you dressed in the morning they were in your cap and after a few minutes you felt them crawling down your face. One night I was fast asleep and was awakened by a loud bumping. When I came to I found my mate in the other bunk hitting them with a hammer, squashing them against the bulkhead. It was a reality that the lads who were emotionally weaker, gradually went to pieces. The strain added to the long absence from loved ones, (often there were marital problems, real or imagined) plus the fact that there didn't seem any chance of a relief to enable us to return to Britain, affected many. Being under tight control everyday niggles added up and were not helped by the high temperatures and humidity. We saw them disintegrating in front of our eyes. I wondered whether it was that or bugs which my cabin mate George had succumbed to. Poor old George!

All this meant that whilst on the empty trip we had to clear everything out of our cabin, unscrew the bunk frames, where we found hundreds of them, scrub it with disinfectant and put everything back again. This was effective and it was heaven to be able to sleep normally – for a while. They soon returned in force.

The cockroaches were another nuisance; they used to gather amongst the electric wiring, which ran in channels in the deck head (ceiling). They were about three quarters of an inch long, fat and heavy. I shall never forget the scream that rent the silence one evening when a Sister came through into the ward and one dropped out of the channelling and straight down into her cleavage. She retrieved it herself!

Bombay, India, 1943, showing "Gateway to India" arch (right).

The sea trip with no patients on board was a pleasant and necessary break. When we were operating normally with the fleet we were very occupied, often with worrying about not yet solved illness, in temperatures which never fell below 84°F in the ward. There was, of course, no climate control apparatus on board. In temperate zones we were cold, in tropical ones we were hot. Whilst I was in charge of the ward my official desk was alongside the sterilisation facility for our ward use. The steam and heat from it was not appreciated.

At about that time the Navy's approach to problems was brought home to me. We were told that there was to be a muster of stores, which meant that each ward was to count and make a return of all the articles issued to it. For example, we were supposed to have six hot water bottles. When I checked I found that we had only three. I was worried because I would be held responsible, due to being in charge of the ward. I went down and spoke to the Chief in charge of the section. "Chief, I've got a problem," I said. "What's that, lad?" I told him that I had three hot water bottles instead of six. "That's no problem, lad," he said.

"Crossing the line" ceremony, 1945.

"Just cut three in half and return them as six defects!" Even though we were at war, the old service attitudes still fought back occasionally. I went back and cut them in half.

There were a few plus points. I shall never forget one evening when I was sitting out in the stern of the ship. All the stars including the Southern Cross, still something of a novelty, appeared so near in the velvety dome of the heavens they were almost sending a message of the greatness of the universe. But the final, marvellous, serene feature was when you looked dead astern and there was the breath-taking tropical moon, low down over the horizon. It was shining directly at us and lighting up the wake, which seemed to follow us all the time as a million little lights. For a while, overcome by the romance of the scene, I was in another world. Then I remembered that we had no women partners to share it with and we were still on a navy ship thousands of miles from home, perhaps just as well!

As we were empty of patients this was the first time we had enjoyed a line crossing ceremony. Before we had been too busy. The ships crew fixed up a canvas tank for us to be ducked in. It was the usual hot day. One of those many days in the tropics when the sun rises as a red ball and you say, "Oh Lord, here it is again." And you know that your clean white shirt and trousers will soon be soaked again in sweat!

All the navy side of the ship were allowed to take part, Officers, Sisters and lower deck. We were, in turn, swished over with a whitewash brush of various coloured soapy lathers and given a promise that Father Neptune would forever afterwards protect us from all the goblins and dangers of the sea. It took you right back to the earlier sailing days and probably was a survival from then. Naturally, the most enjoyable part was before and after your own ducking when you could laugh and cheer the others, especially the Matron and Sisters, some young and attractive, others older and regal. In our state they were all desirable, if only you could have said so!

We sailed on and on, enjoying the sight of the many birds, fish and whales, each in its own way fascinating. Especially the flying fish gliding along just above the water and the marvellous albatross also gliding, often for days on end, just above our stern flagpole, patiently waiting for gash (waste) to be thrown over board from our galley. I loved to watch them collect it from the water. They glided down, quite slowly, to pick it up in their beaks and often landed on the water in doing so. Their wings were so long they appeared to double fold them, firstly the tip bent under about a third of the full length and then the rest of the wing. Frigate birds and terns also accompanied us, oh so delicately beautiful!

We saw beautiful sunsets whilst travelling down the coast of India. They were quite magnificent, made especially so because being in the tropics the sun set more quickly than at home. This made the colours and the cloud patterns change whilst you watched, and it was truly magnificent. The whole range of visible colours were drifting and shooting and fading for the whole sunset period.

Eventually we reached Ceylon and anchored in the main port, Colombo. We were a step further east, where the atmosphere was quite different to our first sample in Bombay. It is difficult to describe but although it was just as crowded it seemed cleaner. The roadside gutters were still what we would call trenches about three feet deep in order to take away the monsoon rain. The people were however of slighter build and their saris more airy. Just a reaction!

We were due to stay in Colombo for only a few days to pick up stores and have any necessary service taken care of. We were, however, given maximum shore leave so that we could do a quick explore. Away from the docks it was pleasant but very hot and more humid than anywhere else we had been before. It is the humidity that you notice most. Your clothes are soaking wet with sweat, you put a clean dry shirt and shorts on to go ashore and in ten minutes you could ring them out again. One notable trip we made was by rickshaw to a nearby Buddhist temple. We hadn't seen many previously and I was quite attracted to its appearance. The Buddha inside was heavily decorated with gold and the place looked cared for. We also managed to go to the Galle Face hotel where they had a swimming pool. This was a special concession and the hotel itself was only available to Officers. We ratings were excluded. This was quite natural for the armed services to practise, but it amused me because one of my aunts had stayed there just before the war when she was on a world cruise. Had I not been in uniform I could have gone in!

Chapter 10

TRINCOMALEE

We soon sailed away to get our permanent berth in Trincamolee. This meant sailing round the southern tip at Dondra Head and then north up to almost the top, where Ceylon abuts India. Trinco, as we always called it, was a small village on the coast, almost lost in a very large inlet that had been taken over by the armed forces. We sailed in through a rather narrow entrance and picked up our berth in the middle of the fleet, which we were to serve as a hospital. During the time I was there it grew larger and larger. There were mainly British ships but we also had French, Italian, Dutch, USA, and almost any maritime country you could think of. It was a very large and gradually increasing number, which made up the British eastern fleet. We were at last home in the sense that this had been our intended job from the beginning. All else before this had been attempts to make use of us on the long journey out. The eastern fleet was gradually working itself eastwards with us acting as the floating hospital, tied up as usual in midstream.

When we had settled down I was to continue to be in charge of the medical ward in which I had gained quite a lot of experience by now, almost all of it in tropical medicine. We still had most of the problems of the pests, collecting naval cases of P.U.O. (Pyrexia of Unknown Origin). Most of them were from soldiers or marines who had been in Burma. There were several occasions when the medical reports were written as capital letters, the ultimate being G.O.K. -God Only Knows, often on the Burma cases.

By this time we were beginning to have food problems. Apart from going down to mess (our meal quarters) to be confronted with a plate of stew of doubtful origin, we also had butter that had gone green around the outside and breakfast porridge full of weevils. We used to flood the bowl with milk, give it a good stir, and skim them off before we could eat it, (and them I suppose)! We found that the meat was some that we had stored at Mombasa nearly two years before. It was forever after known as Mombasa camel! Technically we could complain in a proper naval manner through the Officer overseeing our mess. We did that and were told that the Officers were the same. Full stop. We didn't, rightly or wrongly, believe that but so what, don't you know there is a war on?

Trincomalee was some six degrees north of the equator. It was hot. We were used to tropical heat by now but we hadn't realised how much higher the humidity could be compared with our previous bases. We soon found out. On one visit to a cruiser to see a mate of mine, they couldn't stay down in the mess deck it was so uncomfortable. They had to go down and fetch their food and come back up and find a shady spot where they could sit. They were also rationed for the use of water. It made us realise how lucky we were. The main trouble, it seemed, was that when the ship had its last refit they put a wooden layer over the metal deck. In the tropics the wood had come away and let the sun beat down on the metal deck under which was the mess.

There was a submarine depot ship anchored nearby. The subs used to come back from spells of duty up towards the Japanese-held areas and tie up alongside like a mother hen and her chicks. There were facilities for the crew to relax and any medical problems were sent to us. One day I was able to get across to it and have a look round, including going down into a submarine. It was fascinating, but grim. You went down the conning tower into the main deck; this seemed to stretch all along the middle of the boat with different departments along each side. The first thing that struck me was the engines occupying quite a length on each side of the walk. They seemed only a few inches from your face. What it must have been like when they were running I couldn't imagine. The various messes, Officer's quarters and ratings were also on one or the other side, with so little space that it was disturbing. At the far end was a ratings mess, just a curtained partition with a table and benches each side of it. They told us that when they wanted to fire the forward torpedoes the tubes had to be pulled out towards the mess, which had to be dismantled to allow it. I was glad to come up the conning tower and get on board the depot ship, and that was when it was tied up with no crew inboard. I just can't imagine what it was like when it was in action. I suppose you get used to anything eventually but it certainly increased my admiration for the men who manned them. On top of all this they had additional health problems in subs in the tropics. When men came on to the hospital ship after a voyage they were covered with all kinds of skin diseases due to the close humid atmosphere and the infrequency of being able to wash.

Before we went back to Tjitjalengka we were invited to a cup of tea and a snack that was a tin of chicken one of the submarines had brought in. They had, it seems, stopped a coastal boat, boarded it and amongst the spoils was the tin of chicken. At that moment I appreciated the submariners for other reasons. I did hear it said that people who volunteered for submarine duty were those who liked a casual life, the opposite of that being a big ship life. Meaning that on a battleship or aircraft carrier you had to observe KR and AI, be properly dressed and submit to full supervision with many higher rank Officers aboard.

It was whilst we were anchored in Trinco that I made a mistake which could have been quite serious. Well it wasn't quite a mistake but it could have turned out so. At 2100 before we went off-duty, there was an Officer's round, performed by whoever was Duty Officer that day. It was greeted, when he came into the ward, with a loud call from me. "Attention in the ward," when all the up patients stood to attention beside their beds and all the bed patients put down any books etc which had been filling in time. There was a dead silence. Normally the Officer walked through very sternly looking to right and left, trying to spot something wrong, such as "Those lifebelts are not stowed very well. Get them done." "Aye, Aye, Sir," I said. I would then say, "All present and correct, Sir" and he would go on his way, probably just as fed up with it as we were. On this one day though I had a problem. Knowing that it was rounds time I checked all I could and counted the number of patients in the ward ready to report to him. This night they were not all present and correct, one was missing. What should I do? I could still report all correct and hope to see him soon. Should he not return, having fallen over the rail and drowned, I'd have had to take the can. If I reported one adrift it would be the Officers responsibility. This was where KR and AI were at odds with sensitivity. I'd rather have covered for the man adrift

Trincomalee, Ceylon, 1944.

and then set about finding him, but I decided it wasn't sensible of me to do that. If you follow the rules you should be all right, so I doubtfully said, "one man adrift sir." That began the use of the system. I'd no idea what I was letting loose. I imagined foolishly, that the Officer would say well he's probably in the cinema, which was on the top deck and send one of my ratings to find him. I should have known better. He simply sent someone out to find him and put the miscreant in his report, which meant that it didn't stop there. The report went to the commissioned ward master who supervised our section, then to the Captain. The next day I was told that the missing man had been found in the cinema. He was being charged with being absent from duty, a dreadful crime, and I would be required to attend the office at 1100 the next day with him. When I checked up I found that the miscreant was a 'Master at Arms'. This was the highest non-commissioned rate and since he was in charge of naval discipline in his area, a man of power. I was genuinely worried by what I had done, wishing I had risked it. The next morning at 1100 we both sat on the bench outside the office waiting to be called, caps on. I said, "I'm sorry about this master, I'd no idea it would

Chinese New Year, Trincomalee, 1944.

84

go this far, I hope it ends well." He looked at me with a strong stare, "So do I lad, for your sake." This didn't help me. I knew he meant it and he could have got almost anything done if he had wanted to. He was called in, the necessary Officers sitting at a table as he was marched in. I sat on the bench waiting in case I was needed as a witness, not very happy with life. Eventually he came out. "You have been lucky son," he said and marched off past me into the ship. Apart from being relieved I was also puzzled. What, if it happens again, was best for me? Should I report it as "all present" and suffer if it went wrong or go through another worry like this? I never did really sort it out. Theoretically I should have reported him and he would have to take the consequences. In practice, if I did anything could happen to me. In the Navy you must learn not to be caught doing anything wrong or, at times, anything right!

There was a groups of WRENS just over the water where a sea inlet came in. We were very strictly instructed that it was out of bounds to us unless we were on duty. We were therefore both delighted and inquisitive when we heard that once a month there was a dance night over there. Quite a fair sized party from Tjitjalengka went, full of hope and expectations. When we arrived we were shown the building in which the dance took place. In we went. There were dozens, if not hundreds, of sailors and about thirty WRENS. If you managed a dance you were lucky. I was lucky or so I thought. A lass named Paddy was there with whom I used to go to dances when I was at Portsmouth, where we had struck up a mainly friendly partnership. She was a lovely girl whose parents kept a tight grip on her when sailors were around. I used to be invited to her house from time to time. She had joined the WRENS after I had left England and had recently been sent to Trinco. Naturally I felt that because of my previous contact I'd be specially favoured as a partner. Not a bit of it. Paddy asked me for two or three dances only during the evening. I was disappointed and became rather peevish – foolishly. Had the situation been reversed I'd have done the same. However we didn't fall out and she also introduced me to her friend Betty, and I soon found that I preferred her anyway! I also found that there wasn't any opportunity to break the rules either. If we weren't in the dance hall, we could go outside onto a shingle beach area. There were some seats there and we were allowed to sit with a girl but sit only! It was heavily patrolled by naval police. Anyone caught smooching was soon put right so far as the regulations were concerned. I found out later that this applied to all the beach areas around the naval base. You could meet a girl for the evening during which, apart from the canteen, there was little else to do. If you decided to sit on the beach, even at the roadside that joined the shingle it was only a few minutes before you were moved on. If the naval police tell you to do or not do something you obey, so we did on the one or two occasions when we tried it. There was simply no opportunity for any partnership to develop and that was the end of it. It was probably felt that if no one was allowed on the beach then Japanese spies wouldn't have anyone to mingle with.

Whilst we were there I met most of the senior Officers. Admiral Somerville and Admiral Mountbatten came aboard from time to time, sometimes to see the Captain and sometimes to see one of the Sisters who were on board. Somerville in particular seemed a pleasant man so far as I was able to judge. I've no idea what they were like, of course, when doing their job.

It was about this time that two or three of us decided that we were getting physically slack as we were not having as much football and cricket as earlier. I was smoking sixty cigarettes a day besides finding time for a few pipes full of tobacco. Normally we used to get up about 0630 so that we had time to get our breakfast and get ready to be on the ward for 0745. We decided to get up at 0600 and give that half hour to fitness. This meant running round the deck, exercises and parallel bar work, using some of the suitable handrails on the ship. This helped and we felt better for it after a couple of weeks. We still didn't give up cigarettes though. Apart from the fact that we were addicted by then, wartime service is a mixture of periods with little to do mixed with times of overwork or danger. We needed them for both. There was nothing to occupy us in Trincomalee off-duty. We could either go ashore and swim or go ashore and drink at the canteen or just go ashore – if we could get a lift. It was just a wartime base for moving over into the pacific for the final stages of the war against Japan.

Whilst at Trincomalee we went by coach to see the Lion Rock at Sigiriya, where we had to climb a stairway up the side of the cliff for 656ft. On the same trip we visited Polonnaruwa, the capital of Ceylon in the 11th and 12th century AD. On another occasion we went to Anhuradhapura, the first capital of Ceylon, dating from the 5th century BC.

At Christmas we had the usual celebrations, which basically meant a concert party and getting drunk. Being drunk was not allowed officially, but there were several degrees of drunkenness before you were in any danger of being found out and it was normal practice that if one of your group was in any trouble or danger the rest helped him out. I must add here that I never saw anyone go on duty in any degree drunk, had they done so they would have soon been found out and in serious trouble. We were invited to watch the stage show put on by the ships company and there were some very good professional-quality acts. In fact, I found that to survive Xmas and New Year celebrations you needed to be a bit drunk. What the Scots couldn't do on New Year's Eve the rest of the ship's company managed at Xmas. There was one occasion when I watched one of my mates drinking beer. He had obviously had much practice. He tipped a full glass down his throat by throwing back his head, followed by the whole lot coming back all down his front when he sat up again. He was literally full up.

It was about this time that our ward Medical Officer was promoted to Senior Medical Officer. This meant that although having overall supervision of medical cases he had to stop being directly in charge of our ward, which in fact was quite a busy one with around one hundred cots in it. A new Medical Officer was sent from the U.K. and eventually arrived. He was a pleasant man so far as naval discipline allowed but unfortunately, though not unexpectedly, he had little knowledge of tropical medicine. He had been told, however, as I found out afterwards that he could rely on my experience and this he did.

I was very happy to fit in and oblige. When he came in to do his rounds on the first morning he admitted that he had no experience of tropical diseases. He had been sent on a seven-week course to one of the schools of tropical medicine before he left the U.K. As I already knew the difference between theory and practice I understood how he felt. It worked out quite well, however. When he first came on the ward I had the records of all those who were fit to leave us ready for him and I went over diagnosis and treatment with him of any which had come in sick since the previous morning. I told him what I thought it probably was and what lab tests we usually did and the subsequent treatment. This he kindly accepted until he gradually gained experience himself. It was a very creditable action on his part. He was an Officer and I just a rating and we were under naval discipline. He could have been pompous and tried to cover up the situation and I could have done little about it. What we used to call "yes sir, yes sir, three bags full sir." Not to their face, of course.

There was one very significant development at that time when penicillin appeared as a new drug, new to us anyway. We had known about it for a little while but it took time to reach us. We had heard of its supposedly marvellous results and were quite excited about it and the chance of using it ourselves. It was in a small glass container and had at that time in its development to be kept in a fridge until used by injection. Our first chance came when we had an admission, one afternoon, of a rating with severe pneumonia and pleurisy. He was very ill and might well have died. The MO decided to use part of our limited stock of penicillin. The injections were given and in due course I went off-duty. When I returned next morning I went straight to the pneumonia case to see if he was still there or had died in the night. To my amazement he was sitting up in bed and reading a magazine. I was speechless. It seemed that a miracle had happened. He had had a chest X-ray when he was admitted which showed clearly the affected area of the lung and there was no likelihood of mistake. We had another one taken and he was almost clear, it was truly remarkable. I was most impressed and thought what a wonderful drug it was and how many lives would be saved. I didn't at that exciting time realise that it would be used unwisely until the bugs which caused the various relevant diseases would mutate and leave it almost ineffective.

On another occasion one of my pals caught VD. This was most unusual, as we had all seen the results of this disease on patients who came in with it. I just couldn't understand how an experienced Sick Berth Petty Officer could take that risk. He was being treated in a separate ward where all such afflictions were sent and I went along to see him. He was very depressed and as is usual he blamed the girl for his trouble. "I never thought the cow would be like that" he said, or words to that effect. I reminded him of his part in the happenings but he didn't really appreciate it.

Normally when the Navy sends you to the Far East the period of service is eighteen months and then a relief is sent and you go home. In war time there is no limit except through necessity. After we had been out for two years we began to talk about our reliefs even though we didn't believe there would be any. The factor that strengthened the idea was that whilst at Trinco we heard at first a vague buzz and then a gradually strengthening belief that we were going to Australia. This set up two groups of ratings, those who wanted to stay on and go to Australia and those who, given the choice, would go home. I was, I am now sorry to say, amongst the go-homers. It didn't make any difference though in the long run. Yes, we did go to Australia. No we didn't get a choice because there were no reliefs. Now, I am very pleased that I went, but a two-year stay away from home is a long while, especially when you were planning to get married. The distance between Ceylon (Sri Lanka) and the UK was enormous and I felt that to go further, in fact as far away as you could be, was depressing. Even then we used to say, "If I get through the war I shall be glad I was in it." That has proved to be true and I am now glad I went to Australia and into the Pacific.

The day eventually arrived and we were told that we were to sail for Australia. Once again we left empty of patients, and once again we had to clean and debug our cabins. I was still in the same one. As a Petty Officer I could move into P.O.'s accommodation, by rights, but there were only so many cabins. All these had been occupied from the beginning and there was no other P.O.'s accommodation. There was a war on and we were helping to fight it. Nothing else mattered.

Chapter 11

MEET THE PACIFIC FLEET
AND SET SAIL FOR SYDNEY

The trip from Sri Lanka to Australia is a long one and it meant that we didn't see land for several weeks. There was, however, plenty of interest when you had time to look. The further south you went the more the change from northern hemisphere to southern was felt. You became used to looking up at the night sky and seeing the Pole Star gradually receding and the Southern Cross with its own constellations becoming dominant. In due course we were sailing to the south of Australia across the Great Australian Bight, that giant curve of the south Australian coast, rather like a southern bay of Biscay only far bigger and much rougher because you were subjected to those big seas that come right up from the South Pole. One day I was off-duty and playing darts with one of my mates. The weather was fine and sunny with a pleasant breeze, a day when you would expect a calm sea anywhere else. In the Bight it was not calm. There were great big rollers coming in from the south, which meant they were rolling up from side to side, a real heavy sea. We had to brace ourselves to counter the roll, but at the same time the dart board which was suspended from a hook by a piece of cord swung in an arc of some four feet in length. We had to set our legs apart, stand and at the same time wait to catch a moving dart board as it reached its central point at 6 o'clock. We managed. There was a war on!

Eventually we came into sight of the Australian coast and turned into the channel between the heads, quite a narrow channel that widened out to what was known as the circular key, the Sydney waterside.

Sydney, Australia! It was difficult to believe we had come so far. There was, however, no escaping the fact that it was almost three years since we left home. During shore leave outings we explored the city. There was a particular store which we visited often and where we had a cup of coffee. In the restaurant was a ladies quintet playing popular tunes. We used to sit near the band and, they soon came to know us. After a few visits I was surprised to hear them, as soon as we sat down, begin to play a tune of the time called "The sailor with the navy blue eyes." This went on for a week or two and was accompanied by much ribaldry from my mates. I never found out who had tipped them off. However we enjoyed it and so, apparently, did they. Of such incidents are memories made. I remember Sydney as a modern town which was nice to visit and very friendly. I found the licensing laws rather peculiar. If you wanted a drink you went into a pub and stood at the bar to drink until closing time, which was 1800. It was said that many Australians called in on their way home from work.

It was quite something to visit the well known surfing beaches such as Bondi and Manley, even though it was calm and gentle at the time, the knowledge that you had been there and seen them was great. I was also lucky enough to have a long weekend in the Blue Mountains at Katoomba. A friendly family had a couple of us and took us around the beauty spots. I was particularly impressed by the view across the Three Sisters Peaks. I'll always remember that with pleasure.

There was a very different attitude to women compared with home. I have a strong memory of being entertained by a Sydney family for a day and sitting out on a seat in the evening with the two sons and just having a drink and talking. The peculiarity was that although there were two very attractive girls with us on the seat they completely ignored their presence and talked all evening about

Sydney Harbour Bridge, Australia, 1945.

90

horses. This was on a balmy, semi tropical night full of romance. Perhaps it was our undoubtedly sex-starved condition that highlighted it but it was still far removed from what we knew as entertaining the fair sex!

At that time there was no opera house and the Sydney bridge was the main landmark. For some unknown reason it has always stuck in my mind that I had been both over and under the Sydney and Forth bridges. Memory is a strange thing.

One day we walked down the red light district of Sydney just to see what it looked like. It was an unimpressive suburb with ordinary, small houses and nothing unusual happening. It felt rather like going into a nightclub at eleven o'clock in the morning. Funny thing, glamour, isn't it?

Eventually it was time to move on. We once again sailed out between the heads into the southern ocean. Our course was between Australia and New Zealand through the Tasman Sea. The weather was fine and warm and we had no patients aboard. We were destined for the Philippines and were following just a few days behind the American fleet, which was gradually approaching Japan. We went through the Coral Sea, of battle fame, to reach New Guinea. Regrettably we were not able to get shore leave and had to be content with looking. It was still interesting, however. These kinds of calls were often because an outlying place needed a specialist doctor who would be sent ashore for a day, or a couple of days, whilst the ship waited. It didn't usually include any sick berth staff, unfortunately. Our route was past the Molucca Islands to the Philippines, which was then occupied by the US forces. I can remember on one occasion after we had been in open sea forages I happened to look through the porthole and there was a palm tree. A palm tree meant land and we hadn't seen any for a long while. Further investigation showed a small tropical island with just one or two palm trees on it. This was to be the pattern of things for the next few days, passing small tropical islands. On we went, eventually leaving them behind.

There is one abiding memory of that time. There were crashed aircraft on almost every island, even the smallest. There had, of course, been a series of battles as the US forces fought their way up the Pacific Ocean towards Japan. There was also a strong naval presence, mainly US ships but including some British and other nations. Temporary airstrips had been made as the islands were taken and air battles fought. Most of the time we were so used to being at war that we rarely thought about it. There were times such as this, however, when it was brought back to us in all its brutality and sadness.

In due course we reached Leyte Gulf. We had been following the fleet about fourteen days behind the battlefront. We were to join the Allied fleet when they made a temporary base and act as their hospital. I found that I wasn't destined to stay long in Leyte. I do remember it, however, as being very hot and humid, definitely the highest humidity of all we had previously met. I did get one run ashore for a few hours in the afternoon. I had intended to swim but the beaches were very limited. We had been put ashore in an area of tall scrub, bamboo and many others. It was above our heads with footpaths worn through it by use. Not knowing where I was and being rather careful I decided that I would scout around just a little, remembering that I might get lost and that the natives might not appreciate their bit of earth having been fought over with a fair amount of damage both material and human. I wondered slowly along a path which led to I know not where and was suddenly confronted by a girl wearing little but a grass skirt. We stared at each other for a few minutes when she turned back to what I assumed was her village. Meeting a real live girl in a grass skirt may seem glamorous. I can assure you that it was not. The girl looked attractive but the grass skirt was not. It was just a mess of grass and similar leaves, shrivelled and unclean which hung limply from her waist down to mid calf level. Not a bit like the beauties that paraded the stage of 'South Pacific.'

Soon after that began a considerable change in my life and outlook. One day I was called to the regulating office. With some anxiety I reported. The chief in charge said, "Petty Officer Woolman your relief is due here shortly. Tomorrow you will be ready to go aboard the Argonaut for passage to Sydney." Just at that moment with my head in a whirl I couldn't think of anything to say except, "Right Chief. Thank you." That kind of exchange was typical of the Navy. There I was right away in the Philippines, having given up all hope of getting home after three years away when suddenly in about half a minute my world was turned upside down and all I could say was, "Right Chief." and all I could do was pack my clothes once again into my kitbag and suitcase and find where my hammock was stowed away.

Tomorrow eventually came and the boat came alongside to take me to the Argonaut, a Dido class cruiser of 5,600 tons. She was a cruiser anchored a bit further along Leyte Gulf. I'd never been aboard her before although she wasn't far away from us. I found that there were about half a dozen lads in the boat from other ships, all going to join the Argonaut. The reason being that she was going to Sydney and from there you could eventually be sent home.

I was aware of this because, when I was told, my Medical Officer was told too and he came to see me. He told me that when I reached Sydney the Illustrious, an aircraft carrier, would be there and she would be sailing home soon. He said, "If you are lucky you may be able to be drafted to it. Here is a letter to the Medical Officer in charge on Illustrious who is a friend of mine. Give this to him, it may be helpful." I was very appreciative of this and thanked him suitably. Eventually I was even more thankful for his help.

When we reached the Argonaut I was rather shaken to find that there was no gang way down for people to go aboard, presumably because it would soon be sailing. We had to climb up a rope ladder that was hung from a boom (a long bar of wood slung out from the side and held by a short cable fastened to the outer end). This cable gave you a certain amount of handhold whilst you walked along the boom to the ship. Naturally I had never done this before because hospital ships always had good access when tied up or anchored. I was particularly anxious when I realised I had also to get my kit bag, hammock and suitcase inboard myself. I was certainly not going to make myself look silly in front of perhaps a dozen ratings who had, no doubt, done it all before. There was another factor too. We were in an inlet and the whole Pacific Ocean was outside. The rise and fall as waves came in made quite a difference! My turn came, I gritted my teeth and climbed up in the manner which seemed best, caught hold of the ladder so that it was facing me edge ways and climbed with one leg on each side. This kept it fairly perpendicular whilst I was climbing it. The top side of the spar was flattened so that you had a foothold about four or five inches wide, which helped.

"Three Sisters", Katoomba, N.S.W., Australia, 1945.

93

Once I had overcome that small problem all went well. I was taken along to my mess and shown where to stow my gear and then to the sick bay where I was introduced to the chief P.O. in charge. The mess was similar to all the Royal Navy situations. There were about sixty men in it, all P.O.'s but not all sick berth ones. I was on my own. The sick bay was quite pleasant. A fair-sized cabin with about six cots in it and all were empty. I had a chat with the chief who said, "That's where I sleep," pointing to one of the cots, "and you can use that examination couch over there." It was a good leather covered couch and very comfortable. "Someone will be able to keep in touch with you in case you are wanted." In fact all of the crew I was in touch with were very helpful. I did have to go into the mess occasionally but mostly only for meals. I didn't know any of the P.O.'s but they were very pleasant and I soon made myself at home.

Of many new routines one was the rum issue each morning. This was made with due ceremony, bugles and the lot, probably not much different to Victory's time. A large drum was brought up and we filed past, each receiving what was known as his tot. There was a set type for each rating. When it was brought up it was rather like treacle and had to be diluted with water. The basic was known as neaters. For Chiefs and P.O.s it was one water and so on down through two water, three water etc. the small tot of neaters according to my reckoning would be equivalent to about half a pint of normal shop rum. You had to drink it on the spot. It was not to be taken away and stored up; this was forbidden. Naturally the challenge being there a fair amount was taken away. Most ratings had a bottle in their locker that was secretly refilled as and when possible. It was forbidden for the reason that it was needed as a good old booze up on special occasions.

There was a good example of stored rum whilst I was on board. One afternoon I went to the mess for supper and there was somehow a different air about it. I was told that one of the P.O.s was due to leave the ship at about 2300 hours for transfer to a small naval base on one of the islands that dotted the area. Everyone felt sorry for him as we were going to Sydney. When I went into the mess for supper they were all sitting round the table cheering him on in an old naval ceremony. When anyone had a special occasion, such as a birthday or a child born, it was celebrated by drinks all round. Everyone brought out the bottle of rum from their lockers, the rum that they were forbidden to store and the man concerned went right round the table, one at a time and took a sip from everyone's glass. This was called sippers. There was another similar ceremony when something really special had happened and the lucky man was allowed to take a drink instead of a sip. This was called gulpers. The effect on the lucky recipient was quite noticeable and if sippers made you happily drunk you can imagine what gulpers did. The Petty Officer concerned was in a state of incomprehension and it was obvious that he had received gulpers. The problem then was that he might be too drunk to be able to go to his draft. That would have meant that he'd have been in trouble and another P.O. would have been sent instead. I was quite worried since that would have been one of the P.O.s in the mess that I was in. I went back to the sick bay after supper and kept my fingers crossed. I heard nothing more about it and so I assumed that all had been well. I expect his mates had worked on him to get him sober. No one was left to suffer if it could be avoided.

I had a fairly uneventful trip down to Sydney and quite soon began to get used to a warship and its more restricted way of life. In fact it was a change that I quite enjoyed. Eventually Sydney came into view and we tied up at the docks. This meant casting steel or ordinary ropes ashore, where someone caught it and placed the loop at the end over the top of the mushroom-shaped bollards lining the wharf. At this time, as you were drifting in, the propellers were usually put into reverse until the drift stopped and you were docked. I remember one occasion when we came in too fast. The very thick cable stretched and stretched and then suddenly there was a bang and it broke. More worrying than that was the fact that it whiplashed back along the wharf at about head height. If you had been standing there it would have cut your head off. Big ships don't have brakes and take a long while to stop!

This visit to Sydney was quite different to the previous one when I was aboard Tjitjalengka. This time I left my ship, the Argonaut, and was sent to the main barracks, HMS Golden Hind. It sounded fine and I was on my way home. In fact it was Sydney racecourse, which had been taken over. The main racecourse stand was HQ, which we were taken to, and then I was allocated to a particular watch and to my quarters, a bell tent which I shared with six other ratings. The only piece of furniture was the tent pole by which it was supported. We had to lean our hammocks against that with the rest of our kit piled on the bit of floor allotted to each; not very pleasant. "Don't you know there is a war on?" That wasn't all though. We heard that some people had been stuck in Sydney for eighteen months whilst waiting to get back to UK. It also rained the whole time I was there. It was heavy, thundery, monsoon type rain that got in almost everywhere. Our tents were not much protection. After two nights I'd had enough, and I'd had time to work things out. I came to the conclusion that I was dispensable. I was on a watch system but had not been allocated any duties and was able to get ashore three out of four nights. I realised that no one bothered whether or not I was actually in HMS Golden Hind and so I booked a space at one of the sailors' homes ashore and slept there every night. It was a risk but I just couldn't face a crowded wet bell tent for an indefinite period. I got away with it. Looking back I suppose I'd agree that I was foolish to risk it when I was going home but it is easier to feel that from a comfortable chair at home than it was at the time. Another illegal action that I took was that instead of giving my papers in to HQ when I first arrived, I decided to hang on to them. The overcrowded arrangements for men in transit both to and from the UK to the Pacific made me think that I'd never see them again if I once loosed them and I had feelings of panic that I'd lose passage home because they'd lost my papers. Eventually, I handed them in when I reached my ship to go home. The only weakness I found was that because of my action there was no record on them of my having been in Sydney. I could live with that.

The first priority when I got ashore was to take the letter of introduction I had been given to the Illustrious. I wasn't able to read it, but I knew it was a recommendation from my M.O. on the hospital ship to his pal who was a Surgeon Commander on Illustrious and if I was lucky it might get me home on her. I went along the dockyard and found where she was berthed, marched up the gangway and was confronted by a leading seaman who was on gangway duty. I explained to him that I had a letter for the Surgeon Commander. I was rather foolishly hoping that I'd be allowed to give it to him, but that was not to be. "Right," said the man on duty, "Give it to me and I'll see that he gets it." Owing to the importance to me I was not happy about that but it had to be and I did so. After that I just had to wait. To my amazement three or four day later I was called into the duty office and told that I had a draft to the Illustrious and there was a lorry leaving for there at midday. I could hardly believe it. I'd achieved in two weeks what could have taken two years!

It was with both pleasure and some trepidation that I walked up the gangway of the aircraft carrier. She was indeed á big ship (28,619 tons) and famous too. However she was going home and I was on her and that was the overriding fact. I learned later from one of the sick berth staff that the number of people trying to get drafted to her was enormous. The reason I had succeeded was the letter of introduction plus the fact that the Petty Officer who's place I had taken, caught VD and didn't want to return home until he was cured. This was lucky for me but not unusual in those days. We were to remain for a further few days and then we sailed - for home! I thought I was dreaming, after three and a half years it didn't seem possible. I couldn't tell my folks and Enid that I was coming because all letters were censored and you naturally weren't allowed to talk about ship movements.

Chapter 12-

ILLUSTRIOUS AND THE TRIP HOME

Life on an aircraft carrier was quite different to being on a hospital ship. Firstly it was a big ship and was run as one. On small ships and boats you lived close to your mates and the Officers, and everything was more relaxed. The big ones were run according to KR and AI and were pusser. That was naval slang for purser, the Officer who put the details into the Captain's policies and thus made them work. Everything that was being done by the book was pusser.

The first problem I came up against was when we had a dummy run call over the speakers for action stations; a dummy run being any form of practice. I was in the sick bay at the time and the Chief in charge took me with him, otherwise I'd never have found my station. Inside, a carrier is a cross between a factory and a large block of flats. Each part is housed in its own section, and alleyways join these up. Ladders, called companionways, then join each level. To get to my station simply meant running for about three to five minutes up and along and down and along until I got there. Never having been there before it was a bit complicated. My main worry was how to repeat the manoeuvre should it happen for real. I expect, like everyone else, I would have managed.

Another time when I managed was when, one day, the Chief said to me, "You were in X-ray at Haslar, weren't you?" "Yes Chief." "Well the Quack (a doctor was always known as the quack, whilst a sick berth rating was always called doc) wants some X-rays done and we haven't a radiographer on board and I told him that you would do it." I swallowed hard because although I had spent about eighteen months there I was a clinical photographer not a radiographer! However in circumstances like that you don't say you can't, you just do it. I thought quickly and said, "OK Chief but you will have to show me the way your machine works; I've never used one of these before." So he did that, leaving the only problem I had to deal with which was the placing of the body to show what was needed. For instance, you mustn't let one bone cover another that is particularly needed. X-rays are all about shadows! I had to take shots of a knee and a dental problem. I knew how to hold a dental film in place because I'd had one taken of myself some time before. You just put it in place, ask the patient to put his finger in his mouth and hold the small patch of film. The knee was a bit more of a problem but with a little faith I placed the leg on the film in a position that I hoped would give a reasonable picture and pressed the exposure button. You have to learn as you go along sometimes. The next problem was that in the small darkroom they had, which I'd never seen anyway, I forgot to set the clock for developing the dental film. Again another bit of quick thinking solved it; you can work under a safelight with X-ray film. I just took them out of the developer, held them up in front of the safelight and took them out when I estimated that they had been developed sufficiently. That was just a matter of photographic experience. All was eventually finished; they were dried and given to the chief who passed them on to the MO. They looked quite good to me as far as exposure and general appearance were concerned, so I went on with my duties and didn't think much more about it. Some three days later when I went on duty the Chief said, "Woolman you are in the MO's good books, the X-rays you took were just what he wanted." Apparently he had tried to get them taken for some time and every time the positioning of the knee was wrong and he couldn't see what he needed. I was pleased, the Chief was pleased and I had enhanced my reputation, which later could ease a few other things. Another example of never say "Can't" in the Navy. You never know!

There was one occasion when I was told that the Captain was to have a haemorrhoid operation and I was to assist the surgeon. It was quite an occasion really and I was a bit nervous. We prepared the small operating theatre that was there and readied ourselves. It was done under a local anaesthetic. I had to hold instruments such as retractors, which hold the opening apart whilst the surgeon went on with cutting the next stage; in fact I was assistant surgeon. Afterwards he told me I'd make a good surgeon.

We also had a sad occasion when we lost one of our patients and, for the first time, I was present at a burial at sea. It consisted of a short service and blessing, the body being draped with a Union Jack. At the appropriate point the body was slipped into the sea and a wreath thrown in, in memory.

The Illustrious was a fine ship and made light work of the job it was sent to do. It was fascinating to hear the tales and see the photographs of the recent action around the Philippines. The Japanese had tried very hard to sink them but had not succeeded. The only time our crew had been worried was when they began to use suicide planes. They used to dive a plane from high altitude straight at the ship. Everyone held his breath and waited. The only defence was to actually hit the plane as it dived down and deflect it into the sea. Very few were hit.

Although we were, in effect, leaving the war zone we still had quite a bit of work to do. A ship of a thousand plus men could always provide some surprises. The heaviest time for the sick bay was about 1730 when the deck hockey was played. It was absolute mayhem. Legs, arms and the rest were damaged, sometimes broken. The game was played with great ferocity and no shin pads.

I found that life on an aircraft carrier was splendid. There was a terrific area of deck space to walk on and you could get near enough to the side to watch the water swirl by. From time to time flying was carried out and the sick berth staff had to be on an alert. It still amazes me that planes can land and take off from a ship with so little trouble. Sometimes one will make a bad landing and go over the side, or hit the island (The high tower-like structure at one side of the deck, where all the ship's control is centred). When you think, however, a plane takes off and flies hundreds of miles to its destination, carries out its allotted duty and then has to fly back again just as far and find a small dot in the ocean and land safely on it. Besides the navigation required there is finally the task of landing on a ship travelling at perhaps twenty knots and often rising and falling four or five feet. When they were taking off a controlling batman, that is a man with two bats one in each hand, used to stand in front of the plane as it taxied along and by raising and twisting his bats told the aircraft what to do. The plane steadied

A felucca on the Suez Canal, 1945.

itself and then roared off into the air, assisted by a mechanical catapult. At the end of the deck runway they slipped down and down and down until just as you felt they would finish in the drink they would have enough airspeed to begin to rise and away they went. When they came back they came in at a high speed, much too fast to stay on the deck, then the hook on their tail caught in the cheese wires built on to the floor of the deck. Within a few feet they came to a virtual stop and they taxied forward a short way and stopped again. Where they finished up there was a large square cut into the deck and this was the top of the lift which took the planes down into the hold, so that as soon as the lift had returned to normal the next plane could be called in followed by the next one and so on. We had great admiration for the slickness with which this was carried out and the fact that planes were called in and were only on the deck for a few minutes.

Our route from Sydney to home was via the Suez Canal, the Mediterranean, Gibraltar and along the west side of Scotland to Rosyth dockyard. Distances in the Australian area are considerable and the first port of call was Freemantle, which even when sailing through the Bass Strait between Tasmania and Australia is about two thousand miles. Our next port of call Aden, the five thousand mile journey was quite a stretch of water. Throughout it all we saw very little other than the sea, although we did go in sight of the Seychelles.

A view across the stern of HMS Illustrious, sailing up the Suez Canal, 1945.

When we reached Aden we dropped anchor just off shore to wait for our turn through the Suez Canal. This was a lifeline during the war with Germany as the alternative route was via Cape Town. I was very struck by the barren mountain coast opposite to Aden, which led into Abyssinia. There seemed to be nothing there but rocks and heat. Eventually it came to our turn and we sailed into the canal. Past Suez it was quite narrow and ships couldn't pass each other. This was why each ship needed careful control, especially ones as large as Illustrious. One thing in particular fascinated me. As we moved slowly through the water there was a bow wave which built up in front of us and then was sucked right down as we went on, giving something like six feet difference in level before and behind, and all the time sucking at the banks. I couldn't help but wonder how they stood it. All the way along we passed Egyptian people on the desert land and many small feluccas being sailed up and down; it was a hive of activity. Just after we passed El Shallofa the canal widened out. This was the Little Bitter Lake, which gave plenty of room for small craft to move around, but still two big ships could not pass. It was like this for about fifteen miles and then quite quickly the canal opened out into a large sheet of water, the Great Bitter Lake. There were many ships of all kinds anchored there, waiting for their turn to pass through. After a fair wait we were signalled through. In fact I think as a warship we must have had some priority. The banks and surrounding country were gradually getting busier as we moved along the last stretch of about sixty miles to Port Said but there seemed to be many square miles of nothing but sand as far as the eye could see. We had by now left behind the Great Bitter Lake. Passing Ismailia and El Quantara we went slowly towards Port Said and the Mediterranean Sea. When we were about two miles from Port Said there was a most noticeable difference in the air. It became so strong that we had to remove the scoops and close the ports. Scoops were home made from empty tins that were made to fit into the portholes with the open end facing toward the direction of the wind when we were at anchor and facing forward when we were sailing ahead. By then the smell was really bad. Later we found that it was from Port Said. It caused much amusement.

We stayed in Port Said long enough for me to have a shore leave. A couple of mates went with me and although it was hot we were used to it and walked around the town viewing the shops and the people. There was plenty there to see. The first event was when a couple of young boys perhaps about ten years old came dashing up. "You want feelthy pictures?" They said, showing us what nowadays would be innocuous. "Run away," was our kind reply. They kept worrying us and eventually one of my mates brought an envelope with several prints inside, sealed up. The kids grinned and ran off. When we opened the envelope there were some quite nice photos of bridges and buildings, not a "feelthy" one amongst them. We hadn't expected anything much different. We went into a shop to buy some souvenirs and we were pleasantly surprised to be invited to sit at a small table whilst we looked at the various old and new objects they were selling. The surprise was the cup of coffee that they offered us. Firstly we hadn't expected it and secondly it was, I suppose, real Egyptian coffee, just like a mixture of honey water and sand. We returned to the ship with some more memories.

Next morning we sailed along the Mediterranean, past Crete and Sicily, remembering the terrific sea and air battles that had been fought there earlier in the war for access to North Africa and to keep Malta in our hands; a very valuable strategic island, later awarded the George Medal for bravery.

We proceeded past Sardinia and the Balearic islands, eventually coming in sight of the rock of Gibraltar. It had been a very agreeable trip along the Med., lovely sunshine all the way. I couldn't help thinking of the climate and heat in, say, Majorca when you came there from England, whereas for us just having left after two years in the tropics Gibraltar seemed to be a pleasant summer day with sun, breeze and blue water.

During a two or three days stop we were able to get a reasonable shore leave. We went up the rock and saw the monkeys and from there looked down on what seemed a very tiny harbour with toy ships in it. The feeling that we were in Britain couldn't be shaken off. You went through the town and across the road was a red GPO type post box. You reached a junction and a policeman in British uniform controlled it; even the currency was like being at home.

We quietly sailed on into the Atlantic, away from land and up the west side of Britain. We couldn't go up the North Sea as there were mines about and so we kept to the west of Ireland and round Malin Head along the west coast of Scotland. It was as good as a cruise except when an occasional four inch gun shook the air with a burst of fire at a floating object, usually a floating box but you have to play safe.

I was very impressed with an excellent view we had of the Giant's Causeway; it was quite magnificent. As we moved further north past the Western Isles it seemed noticeably cooler and to us cold. But it was still a beautiful day, calm sea and beautiful sunshine even as we moved round Cape Wrath and along the north of Scotland. Although it was rather barren and thinly populated it appealed to me and I made a mental note to try to visit one day. As yet I haven't managed it! Our route took us through the Pentland Firth between the Orkney

Islands and the Isle of Stroma. As we approached the Pentland Firth the ship began to roll considerably. I happened to be on deck and suddenly realised that what had been a smooth calm sea must have turned into a roughish one, yet there was still no wind so why was it behaving like this? We'd been through quite rough and rolling seas and yet this felt different. I walked towards the side of the ship and looked down from somewhere amidships and the sea was still calm but absolutely boiling. Circular currents, long flowing currents, everything you could think off. It was this that was causing the roll. I realised that it was the north Atlantic flowing along into the North Sea through the comparatively small outlet of the Pentland Firth that was causing the movement. It is remarkable how conditions of that kind can swing a ship as large as the Illustrious about.

At last we turned south and went comfortably down the east coast of Scotland, into the Firth of Forth and under the bridge to Rosyth. You can imagine my state of mind, it was October 1942 when I last saw Britain and when I looked over at the dockyard I saw the usual rail lines but I suddenly realised that if I went along one of them there would be a direct line to home. In fact it took me some time to believe it! There were, however, still many things to be done before I was free. I was still in the Navy.

Chapter 13-

ARRIVE AT ROSYTH

The first thing I did was to ring home and then another call to Enid. Her immediate reaction was, "I'm coming up to see you. Please get me somewhere to sleep." I tried to explain to her that in wartime there was little accommodation available but couldn't shake her. The next afternoon, when I went ashore I took a train to Edinburgh to try to find a bed for her and eventually was lucky. The next day I met her at the station. It just didn't seem real after three and a half years away.

The next excitement was when we were told that we were due to be transferred to our depot next day. That meant HMS Victory, Portsmouth. Before we could take our belongings ashore we had to clear customs. Instead of us having our goods examined at the gate the customs men came aboard and we gave them a list of anything we had that needed clearance. They were very good and charged us only a token amount each. Next morning away we went to the station in Edinburgh over the Forth Bridge to Inverkeithing where we met the main line train to England. I met Enid at the station and she travelled down with us. After a long, slow journey we reached London where we crossed over to Waterloo station and Enid took the train to Winchester and King's Somborne.

On this occasion I was only at barracks for a couple of days and then left for six weeks leave, gratefully received. I decided to go down to Enid's at King's Somborne for two or three days so that we could arrange the wedding before going home. We had decided that this was the best time to have it, as we weren't likely to have a long leave like that again. This done I rang home and told them the details. It was a bit difficult. Kings Somborne is about eleven miles from Winchester. The florists couldn't deliver the bouquets because they had no petrol available. We could not get a photographer and we weren't allowed to have icing on the cake because of the sugar ration. Many people during the war solved this by having a cake and enclosing it in a wooden box made to look like icing. In our case the restriction was eased just before the wedding and so we were not troubled. I took the photographs myself and the bouquets were made by one of the ladies who lived in the village. All went well and my family travelled down with me the day before. We all stayed at the Cricketers, a pub in the village. My best man was a mate of mine, Arnold Kemp.

The morning of Aug 11th 1945 was warm and sunny as two young men walked along the High Street, King's Somborne; both looking a little apprehensive. They were both in the Royal Navy's uniform of a Sick Berth Petty Officer. As they walked together, in step they appeared smart, efficient and capable, in tune with that lovely sunny morning; as they should since Britain and it's Allies had just won the long six-years war against Germany and her Allies. Why then should they seem apprehensive? SBPO Jack Woolman and SBPO Arnold Kemp were both heading for the church in King's Somborne, a few miles from Winchester. The former was shortly to marry Enid Goffe, of King's Somborne, and the latter to assist him as his best man. I still remember the feeling as I walked down the length of the village with Arnold to reach the church. I felt as if every curtained window had someone behind peering at me. They probably had!

As is often the case, Jack and Arnold had to wait in the church for Enid and her bridesmaids – Doreen Woolman, Margaret Shaw (a VAD friend) and Penelope Drew, a smart little girl from the village. The ceremony duly ended, Enid, now Woolman instead of Goffe, and Jack left the church and were honoured by a gathering of VAD friends and Lieutenant Commander Young RNVR from Collingwood, all lined up in their uniforms.

After the reception we left for our honeymoon. I made one fatal mistake. Enid and I went across the road to her home Winton Cottage to change and we drove back to the reception at the village hall to say good-bye. It was a very hot sunny afternoon and I foolishly opened the car roof. We stopped at the hall, said cheerio, and were just about to drive away when someone dropped a large bag of confetti through the roof. It seemed to half fill the car and made us both embarrassed. It was, in effect, a notice that said, "Just married." We had to stop outside King's Somborne and pick out each piece we could find. That evening we were due to stop at Oxford and stay for a week. Everything was fine and we were happy, except that I was quite ill with tonsillitis. I'd had it for a week and it was beginning to get worse. The next morning I managed to get out and have a walk round with Enid but by the end of the day it was obviously getting serious. The landlady was also getting anxious because she had other visitors at the end of the week. I remember telling Enid to go and have a walk round and enjoy herself. She, of course, stayed in with me whilst I stayed in bed. The doctor came, gave me some antibiotics and all became well again. Somehow my friends misunderstood when they asked me, "Where did you spend your honeymoon?" and I replied "in Oxford, mostly in bed!"

These days Oxford doesn't seem such a suitable place for a honeymoon, hardly in the same league as the Seychelles or others but in 1945 and with the war against Japan still going on we were lucky to find anywhere to stay and even more fortunate to have petrol to drive about. For instance my sister Doreen had been trying for two years to have a holiday and had only just managed to arrange it. As it turned out our wedding stopped her going, which was rather unfortunate but in those days we didn't know what today would bring never mind tomorrow! The second week of our honeymoon was spent in the Cotswolds at Chipping Campden. It was there that I began to take an interest in the wild flowers, which were everywhere around us when we went for a stroll. The local bookshop had a book on naming wild flowers, I bought it and we spent most of the remaining days using it. The rest of the leave we spent split between my folks and Enid's. That part of Hampshire in the Test valley was then a naturalist's paradise. It had not been spoiled and orchids were on the downs and rare plants and birds everywhere, even a Bittern in the riverside reed beds.

Eventually the long leave came to an end and we both had to return to our base. I went as usual to Portsmouth barracks and Enid to her VAD HQ in Portsmouth. Within a couple of days I had notification of a draft to HMS Boscawen, which was the Fleet sick quarters at Portland harbour near Weymouth. I was very pleased with this, as I knew I might have been sent out East again. In fact had the atom bomb not been dropped and the Japanese war continued I expect I should have been. There has been a good deal of argument and criticism of the Allies for the loss of life but had we not have done so the war would have continued much longer and the loss of life when we took Japan would have been at least as bad.

In a couple of days I made my way down to Portland and found that I was to be Petty Officer in charge. This pleased me, as it would give me a different experience to the one I had learned on the tropical medicine ward on Tjitjalengka. There were about six other ratings under me. Most of our work was similar to an ordinary doctor's surgery. We took care of the many warships that anchored in the harbour and the various land bases in the area. Very bad cases were sent to the nearby hospital.

Enid had applied for demobilisation, which was available to married women now that the war had ended. This went through quite quickly and we decided to try and find a flat in Weymouth. She came down and we wandered along the front and found one quite quickly, which we rented. It was once a boarding house but during the war had changed to a letting. Just a little past the clock tower on the harbour side, it was just what we wanted. I used to go in to work each morning along Chesil Beach in the bus, quite a difference to being on the Illustrious. I found that the sick berth attendant who had been doing the dispensing had recently been drafted and there was no one else who knew how to do it. I had to do it myself. Although I had passed my exam I didn't know much about it either. Eventually another man came to replace him. I asked him if he had any experience with dispensing. He said he had, so I told him that that was one of his jobs and "if you have any problems ask me." He didn't have anything to ask, to my relief. It was quite interesting to get used to the change in type of jobs to those I had been used to on the ship, sore throats, hangovers, injuries from fighting when drunk (especially at Bank Holidays, Xmas and any other special celebration days).

Time went steadily by and Xmas passed and on New Year's Eve we went to a dance in Weymouth. I remember it well because we found we had left our door key at home. Fortunately there was a top window left open and I was able to climb in. I often wonder what would have happened had the naval patrol come

Jack and Enid, Wedding photograph, Aug 11th, 1945.

by and seen me, a slightly inebriated sailor climbing through a window at one o'clock in the morning.

We enjoyed our stay in Weymouth. It was more like having a civilian job than being in the Navy, though I felt we had earned it. There was not much happening because all thoughts of visiting the seaside had been put on hold during the war. In fact, after a few months we used to walk along the road to do some shopping and never think of glancing over to see if the sea was still there.

We took the opportunity of visiting around since we had the car there, but I was still away at the sick bay for most of the time. At least I didn't have any of the pressures which running the nursery business entailed when I did get home. Our sick bay was situated just inside the dockyard gates on the quayside. We sometimes used to catch shrimps that were swimming just below and eat them for tea.

Eventually I was demobbed. Just like my return from the Philippines it came suddenly. I suppose everything in the Navy did. You know nothing about it until it happened and then you were always in a rush. I remember it was my duty weekend and I was sitting at my desk doing some paper work when a message arrived on the Saturday afternoon saying that I was to proceed to Portsmouth RN barracks for demobilisation. I could hardly believe it. From March 1940 until May 1946 I had been under naval discipline. Woolman PMX 65063 "Sir!" Now I was about to be Jack Woolman again. From twenty years of age to twenty six years is an important piece of your life. It had put a stop to any ideas of advancing in sports, but gave me a terrific boost in self-confidence and belief in myself.

Chapter 14

HINDSIGHT

It has often been said, and even now is believed by many, that the German people must have allowed and even encouraged Hitler. They thought that it couldn't occur in Britain; that we would never allow a dictator to take over in the way in which Hitler did. I have never believed that. I feel that there are a sufficient number of people in Britain of similar inclination to take advantage of any chance that might occur. Hitler did not 'take over' Germany; Hindenberg, who was president, gave it to him. Hitler and his party were elected to the Reichstag and they manipulated things so that Hindenberg made Hitler Chancellor. Hindenberg was an old man and when he died Hitler decreed that he, himself, would be both President and Chancellor. Thus Germany became a dictatorship and a one-party state. The danger here must always be guarded against, even to the point where the originator of the structure means well. The problem develops when some later person exploits the situation. Hitler was the 'later person.' He stirred his people by blaming anything he could onto the Jews. It is worth pointing out that he had quite a following in Britain and other countries. Soon he was all-powerful in Germany – largely attained by letting the SS shoot anyone they liked (and anyone they didn't like!)

I have always felt that I am one of the lucky people old enough to remember life both before and after the war. I was nineteen at the beginning and twenty-six when demobbed. I have seen so many changes during my life. Many of the changes if not most, led from the war. War speeds up development. For example, our first entertainment was provided by a crystal radio set feeding two headphones, one for Mother on one side of the fireplace and the other for Father on the other side. The signal was so weak that should you rustle a newspaper whilst they were trying to hear the radio, you were quickly told to hush. My life now includes radio, and colour pictures from far out into the universe. At the touch of a button I can watch colour TV pictures of events from the other side of the Earth.

What of the effect it had on my generation? I had been brought up in a strict pre-war attitude. The class system was strong and etiquette was important.

My mother and father were strict and I did as I was told. Before the war I was eighteen and it was still expected that I should be in by 10pm. I didn't like it but I knew that it was expected of me and I obeyed. After I had been in the Navy six months I remember my mother remarking, "You aren't my little boy any longer" and I said, "Of course I'm not. You can't expect me to be." Quite quickly I had changed from part of a family, controlled by its head, to a person with his own rights and opinions. Never again could my parents expect to have personal control of my activities. This may have been partly due to my growing older, but I'm quite certain that I would have been very much older before I had succeeded had I stayed at home. I had always been discouraged from visiting public houses and taught to handle drink with care. This stood me in good stead as I became older but the important thing about the war was that I could break my home ties as and when I wanted or needed to. I could get fairly legless and so long as I managed to get on board and below decks, no one except my mates knew about it – and they had helped me to achieve it anyway! There was one occasion when I went to visit my mate on the supply ship and came away with a bottle of gin, for which I paid him five shillings (twenty five pence). My folks at home had no knowledge of it and so no responsibility for it. I often wonder what problems similar behaviour at home would have brought upon me! I was allowed to mature on my own "carrying the can" (naval slang for taking the consequences).

I'm convinced now that humans are built to fight and I am also sure that we were right to stand up to Hitler and his Nazis. There comes a time when you have to make a stand for freedom and democracy. Men such as Hitler cannot be appeased and will continue as long as you let them.